A Holy Haunting

ADVANCE PRAISE FOR
A HOLY HAUNTING

"*A Holy Haunting* makes a compelling case for faith for a new generation! In his winsome and self-deprecating style, Sam D. Kim wins over the seeker and uplifts the believer. It's the perfect book to give to a friend struggling in their Christian faith or a skeptic questioning its veracity. Don't miss it!"

Lee Strobel, *New York Times* bestselling author of
The Case For Christ and Heaven.

"Modern evangelism can at times sound plastic and clichéd, rather than like a genuine conversation. By contrast, *A Holy Haunting* was written as if it were a personal letter to a friend who is sincerely investigating the claims of Jesus. Sam D. Kim shares the gospel with a light-hearted sense of humor and a masterful subtlety that is both authentic and winsome. He doesn't shake, push or sell the gospel as if it were a product; rather he speaks of Jesus as a good friend with whom he had just met for afternoon tea."

Craig S. Keener Ph.D., author of the bestselling
IVP Bible Background Commentary: New Testament,
and co-editor of the award-winning,
The NIV Cultural Backgrounds Study Bible.

"Haunting. A Holy Haunting. All around us. All the time. And Sam D. Kim gets it. And then helps us, wherever we are in the journey of faith, to also get it. The Haunter has wonderfully gifted Sam to open it all up to us through pithy stories, engaging humor (I laughed out loud a number of times!), penetrating cultural insights, and brilliant theological reflections (like dude, how can such a young thinker already see all this?). When I finished the book, my heart was alive in a fresh way, and I found myself longing for Sam's follow-up book. For there will be more to share as the Haunter takes ever greater hold of Sam's amazing mind and gracious heart."

Rev. Dr. Darrell W. Johnson, Fellow at Regent College and author of *Experiencing the Trinity* and *Prolific Discipleship on the Edge: Expository Journey through the Book of Revelation.*

"There are few books where you need to make sure you always have a highlighter or pen at hand. Sam D. Kim's *A Holy Haunting* is one of them. You're certain to come across a line or passage that catalyzes an overhaul of perspective. Like these simple but profound statements: "Abba sees only Lost and Found. These are the only labels that heaven counts." It is a truism that has stuck with me for some time and begs us to wonder, where else might we need to rethink how God sees us and how we see ourselves?"

Bill High, Forbes Nonprofit Council, Founder of The Signatry, Co-author of *Leadership Not by the Book* and *A Generous Life.*

"*A Holy Haunting* befriends the doubter, challenges the church-goer, and gives fresh vision to our earnest questions. Sam D. Kim gives us all–skeptics and believers alike–a roadmap to discovery and wonder."

Benjamin Doolittle MD MDIV, Professor of Religion and Health, Yale Divinity School, Director for the Program for Medicine, Spirituality, and Religion at Yale School of Medicine.

"*A Holy Haunting* reframes our thinking, ignites our imagination, and invites us into deeper and important conversations for this generation and century. Sam D. Kim's profound insights leave us lingering and desiring for more. These pages are filled with such beauty, empathy and wonder that I could hardly put it down!"

Samuel E. Chiang, Executive Director, Global Evangelism Network, World Evangelical Alliance and Co-founder and CEO, Global Center for Giftedness.

"*A Holy Haunting* captures the pressing struggles of contemporary life against the ever-present eternal backdrop of humanity's deepest longing. Sam D. Kim explores the shape of the human soul and our universal search for meaning with the insightful rigor of an academic, the heart of a pastor, and the wonder and imagination of an artist. He combines the witty yet profound musings of a Frederick Buechner with the weighty yet accessible writings of a C.S. Lewis. *A Holy Haunting* is sheer brilliance, and no doubt will become a spiritual classic for the ages."

Rev. Dr. Greg and Canon Carrie Headington, The Lombardi Humanitarian Award Recipient '17, Board Member and Visiting Professor at Fuller Theological Seminary.

"*A Holy Haunting* is a fresh, insightful, humorous, well-researched and gentle guide that will not only stretch your thinking, but ultimately draw your heart toward its deepest longings."

Dr. Steve A. Brown, President, Arrow Leadership and author of *Jesus Centered—Focusing on Jesus in a Distracted World.*

"*A Holy Haunting* is a refreshing look at spiritual longing for our world today. As we shifted to a post-industrial and post-modern society, Sam D. Kim engages us with a smorgasbord of promptings, some of which are fascinating and new, illuminating a quest to fill that 'God shaped vacuum' that Pascal put on our radar. You'll enjoy Sam's style which is witty, fun and insightful, and you'll find yourself pondering what might this quest look like for you. Join him on the journey and see where it takes you!"

Rev. Joseph W. Handley, Jr., Ph.D., President, Asian Access, Catalyst for Leadership Development, Lausanne Movement.

"*A Holy Haunting* reminds us that negation of God does not eliminate the universal human need for transcendence. By pointing us to the deep longings of the human heart—belonging, purpose, truth, meaning, wholeness—Sam D. Kim persuasively points us to the One who can meet our longings. If you find yourself deconstructing your faith, in a place of deep doubting, or just want to strengthen your faith, pick up *A Holy Haunting* and drink deeply."

J. R. Woodward Ph.D., Co-founder of Missio Alliance, National Director, V3 Church Planting Movement, Author of *Creating a Missional Culture*, and co-author of *The Church as Movement.*

"*A Holy Haunting* feels like the 21st-century version of *Mere Christianity*. Sam D. Kim has given us a great gift in this well-researched and crafted work. His research extends well beyond theology and the Biblical text. He understands our culture and the times in which we live and minister. It will help those who already know Jesus be more effective. It will help those who have yet to encounter Jesus find their way home."

Dr. Ron Walborn, Vice President
and Dean of Alliance Theological Seminary.

"*A Holy Haunting* will swoop you in, and before you realize what's happening, it will teach you eternal truths that will transform your perspective and your life! Even if you don't consider yourself a person of faith, you will be better because of it. As Sam D. Kim explains, we are all spiritually hungry, it just manifests in divergent ways. Wherever you may be in your faith journey, *A Holy Haunting* will help you find your way home."

Matt Brown, Founder of Think Eternity
and Author of *Truth Plus Love.*

"*A Holy Haunting* offers an enduring vision of faith amidst the tides of change in a postmodern world. Blending together insight from science, sociology and theology, Sam D. Kim invites both the skeptic and traditional believer into a deeper journey of meaning, purpose and authenticity. A Holy Haunting integrates the head, the heart and the feet into a vision of the human journey, he calls us all to migrate back home to our true selves and

to set our sights on the land of genuine freedom, deep connect-
edness and spiritual communion."

Rev. Daniel Groody C.S.C, Ph.D.,
Associate Professor of Theology and Global Affairs,
Vice President and Associate Provost for Undergraduate
Education at the University of Notre Dame and
the recipient of the '07 Pax Christi USA Book Award

A HOLY HAUNTING

Why Faith Isn't a Leap but a Series of Staggers
from One Safe Place to Another

SAM D. KIM

NASHVILLE

NEW YORK • LONDON • MELBOURNE • VANCOUVER

A Holy Haunting

Why Faith Isn't a Leap but a Series of Staggers from One Safe Place to Another

Published in New York, New York, by Morgan James Publishing. Morgan James is a trademark of Morgan James, LLC. www.MorganJamesPublishing.com

Proudly distributed by Ingram Publisher Services.

Morgan James BOGO™

A **FREE** ebook edition is available for you or a friend with the purchase of this print book.

CLEARLY SIGN YOUR NAME ABOVE

Instructions to claim your free ebook edition:
1. Visit MorganJamesBOGO.com
2. Sign your name CLEARLY in the space above
3. Complete the form and submit a photo of this entire page
4. You or your friend can download the ebook to your preferred device

ISBN 9781631959905 paperback
ISBN 9781631959912 ebook
Library of Congress Control Number:
2022940471

Cover Design by:
Henry Kim

Morgan James PUBLISHING **Builds** with... **Habitat for Humanity®** Peninsula and Greater Williamsburg

Morgan James is a proud partner of Habitat for Humanity Peninsula and Greater Williamsburg. Partners in building since 2006.

Get involved today! Visit MorganJamesPublishing.com/giving-back

For Mom and Dad.

*Sometimes when I miss my parents dearly or feel a little lost,
I come back to my old neighborhood and imagine myself
walking through the doors of our former Manhattan apart-
ment in Inwood. It's ironic; the older I get, the more I look for
my parents. Now that I've been mugged by reality, it's liber-
ating to remember what it felt like to be loved and supported
unconditionally. For me, the gates of heaven will be entering
that door once again and going home.*

Contents

Acknowledgments

To my dearest wife and best friend Lydia, you are my home. Only next to you can I lay my head to rest and find peace in this life. Thank you for all the support you gave during this project—the endless coffee, snacks, and sweet kisses in between—but most importantly, your patience. To my boys Nathan and Josh, I know Dad is always on the computer from dawn to dusk, but I couldn't wish for any other type of noise than the beautiful cacophony only you guys can orchestrate around the house! But don't you worry boys, one day soon when you're recording your next album (Nathan) or writing your next novel (Josh) I will get you both back with a vengeance!

To Leighton Ford, you will always be a real-life superhero to me. There are very few who could rival what you've done in accelerating global evangelism in both depth and scale. Yet perhaps your singular legacy is in mentoring others. You have strived in every way to deflect attention away from yourself and pointed others only to Jesus. Thank you for writing this gracious foreword, but more importantly, thank you for representing our heavenly father so well and giving our generation a Jesus-centered model—to be led more by, to lead more like, and lead more to Jesus—for this is your magnum opus! In addition, I also want to thank so many of my incredible friends and mentors that I admire so much who endorsed this book, you all made me blush and shed a few tears.

To my editor, Margaret Whibley, like Stephen King often says, when it comes to writing, the editor is always right. To write is to err (as you know too well!) and to edit divine. Thank you for faithfully being my steady hand for the last few years. To my agent, Tom Dean, thank you for taking this wild journey with me! You were certainly an answer to my prayers in making this book a reality! To my dear 180 Church family, without you, there is no book. You are my muse and the living letters on these pages! You've taught me that everything else is trivial in our lives compared to our relationships! It is such an honor for me to be given the privilege to do life and ministry with people I love so dearly.

Foreword

A while back, Sam called me and said that some "influencers" wanted to spend a day with me. "What are 'influencers?'" I asked—a clear indication of my age and generation! He explained they are young leaders who use their social media platforms to spread the good news of the gospel. "Many of them have millions of followers," he told me.

"Why would they want to visit me?" I asked. "I don't know much about social media."

"Leighton," he said, "they deeply admire who you are and all that you've done for God's kingdom. And they want to learn from your life and experience across the years from preaching the gospel to millions of people on every continent alongside your brother-in-law, Billy Graham,,, and then starting a new work in mentoring younger leaders from all around the world."

I was intrigued but still wondering how I could be of help. So they came, a half dozen men and women with open hearts. And I have to say: I liked them! I loved their vision, ingenuity, and strong desire to make Jesus known to their generation.

xviii | A HOLY HAUNTING

They reminded me of myself at their age with my fellow evangelists in Youth for Christ. We had a passion to spread the gospel in our generation. I learned a great deal from these influencers that day and have been learning since.

Now I have the privilege of recommending A Holy Haunting in which Sam provides a compelling and beautiful invitation of the gospel to a new generation.

This generation by and large has either been ignorant of or turned off by churches. They're seen as full of judgment rather than grace, with more arrogance than humble faith. And yet those same detractors of the church are still "haunted" by a deep longing for the very source of beauty, truth, and goodness.

We are often told that we live in a "secular" age, where there is neither interest nor need for the divine. Yet according to the influential Canadian philosopher Charles Taylor, we live now in a "cross-space" which is haunted by the past, disillusioned by the present, and without much hope for the future. But even so, Taylor believes secularization today is being more and more challenged.

If so, then the time is right for a new cadre of evangelists and apologists, like Sam and his friends, who believe there is a wide and deep soul-scape open to the authentic Christ.

Sam has intriguingly included in one volume a spiritual memoir, an apologetic for the truth, and a call to a beautiful life in all its fullness. I believe this book will be a helpful guide both for those lured by a "holy haunting," and those already on the path who want to invite others to join them.

Leighton Ford, Honorary Lifetime Executive Chair,
Lausanne Movement Founding President,
Leighton Ford Ministries Charlotte, North Carolina

Introduction

"My coming to faith did not start with a leap
but rather a series of staggers from what
seemed like one safe place to another."
Anne Lamott

SOMEWHERE BETWEEN SKEPTICISM, BELIEF AND WONDER

I remember the first time I saw fireflies. I stood gazing in wonder at an incandescent beam that seemed to radiate from a distance one beautiful summer night in Central Park. For a moment, it was as if Van Gogh's Starry Night—which is on display at the Museum of Modern Art just a few miles from where I was standing—literally came to life right before my eyes. I always found it fascinating that Van Gogh painted that masterpiece from the balcony of an insane asylum in a former monastery in France. For on nights like these, it would have been lunacy not to believe something greater lay beyond the horizon of the well-lit skyline. Most consider *The Starry Night* to be Van

Gogh's magnum opus, and as a child, I deemed God condensing the stars into fireflies as his.

A skeptic may dismiss my memories as childish nostalgia and *The Starry Night* as a byproduct of a self-committed man off his meds, rather than some celestial silver lining displaying God's handiwork. Perhaps the only reason you're reading this opening is because a friend gave it to you, and you don't want to offend them by refusing. You can rest assured that I am no snake-oil salesman peddling religion for profit. For if I was, I would hardly have given up my dream of becoming the president of a major research university—after being accepted into an Ivy League doctoral program ranked first in the country—to instead dedicate my life to the local church. Some may think squandering such an opportunity was madness, but at least now you know selling snake oil is not the only job I qualify for.

I was a skeptic too once, although not about religion. God wasn't a mystery just yet, but girls certainly were. In the third grade, I became convinced that those long-haired aliens must have crashed into earth's orbit from a galaxy far, far away. I then heard the most absurd thing in Sunday School: God created Eve to be a helper! This was entirely contrary to my experience, because none of the girls I knew were at all helpful. They even refused to join in our daily burping contest at recess, calling it "gross." So, I struggled with my first bout of agnosticism. Maybe God had made a mistake. "Helper? Not in a million years!"

My skepticism lasted till the sixth grade, when, ironically, it was suddenly transformed into idolatry. It was befuddling. I learned that a ten-year-old boy was no match for the power of puberty, even though I had a green belt in karate. My agnosticism turned to Jell-O and I found myself undone. From then on, my entire reason-for-being was split into two simple functions: 1) getting a girlfriend, and 2) everything else.

A year out from college, there I was on a beach on my knees beneath a beautiful summer sunset, getting ready to propose to my college sweetheart. I told her to close her eyes until I said she could open them again. I took out the ring to make sure everything was in order, only to see it drop into the sand and vanish without a trace. Gasping for air I plummeted into the sand. I felt like big bursts of sobs might be the correct response, but I held on to my composure because I knew I had to find that very expensive ring. Meanwhile, my girlfriend, unaware of what had just happened, kept asking petulantly if she could open her eyes yet (still not very helpful…). To cut a long story short, I found the ring and she said "yes!" Catastrophe was averted, and there was a wedding and a feast. With the wisdom of hindsight, I learned that my assumptions in third grade said more about my ignorance than about the laws of human nature. That is the story of how I went from being a skeptic to a worshipper. I, who had once scoffed at the very idea of love, was now at its altar.

In the Gospels, Jesus says on one occasion that to enter the kingdom of heaven, we must be born again spiritually; and on another, he says that we must become like little children. In many ways, spiritual rebirth is like the tumultuous changes that occur during puberty, except this time around, the change takes place in the inner workings of the soul rather than the body. This is why I refer to this transformative developmental process as "Spiritual Puberty" since it closely mirrors physical adolescence. If salvation can be compared to birth and puberty, then salvation is always going to be something of a mess. C. S. Lewis, addressing the irony, the conundrum, and often the messy complexities of the faith journey, writes:

> The world does not consist of 100 percent Christians and 100 percent non-Christians. There are people (a great many of them) who are slowly ceasing to be Christians but who still call themselves by that name: some of them are clergymen. There are other people who are slowly becoming Christians though they do not yet call themselves so. There are people who do not accept the full Christian doctrine about Christ but who are so strongly attracted by Him that they are His in a much deeper sense than they themselves understand.[1]

This book is about how we have fundamentally misunderstood the Christian faith at its core and how to reclaim it. A dangerous theological distortion in the church has divorced the sacred from the secular, dividing believers and the unbelievers into an "us" and a "them." Perhaps this is the result of identity politics, or perhaps it is because of the tribal thinking that permeates our culture today, but it is certainly not biblical. At the heart of God there are no liberals or conservatives, blue states or red states. There aren't even Christians or atheists. He sees only Lost and Found. These are the only labels that heaven counts.

At the same time, this dichotomy has created a spiritual void in the broader culture that is proving to be destructive. The sacred and secular divide has led to another dangerous distortion. Developing physically (biologically) and emotionally (psychologically) are deemed essential to human flourishing, yet our post-Christian society has excluded the spiritual dimension.

According to Harvard psychologist Robert Kegan, the critical unfolding of human growth unpacks the lifelong evolutionary longing for balance between inclusion and embeddedness of an organism and its environment (biology) and between the self and the other (psychology).[2] He neglects the spiritual longing and tension that arises from this critical process, however. Consequently, to help bring clarity and provide a focused introduction to the nature of faith, this book will explore faith from three vantage points—theory, process, and practice—offering a robust and all-encompassing overview of biblical faith.

In addition, I realize that the integration of an evolutionary framework with spiritual development may raise a few questions. Chapter five will explore in much greater detail how God uses the process of evolution in creation, however. For the sake of brevity, I'll provide a short summary here. Dr. Francis Collins, director of the National Institute of Health and the founder of Biologos—a Christian advocacy group that supports the view that God created the world using evolution—coined the term "evolutionary creation" as a Christian position on origins. The Biologos Foundation posits:

> Evolutionary creation takes the Bible seriously as the inspired and authoritative word of God, and it takes science seriously as a way of understanding the world God has made. Evolutionary creation includes two basic ideas. First, that God created all things, including

human beings in his own image. Second, that evolution is the best scientific explanation we currently have for the diversity and similarities of all life on Earth.[3]

The first part of the book explores faith in theory. What is faith exactly? Chapter 1 offers a clear definition of biblical faith as a lifelong evolutionary longing to make meaning of human existence in light of a higher plane of reality. It then explores many of the negative ailments that plague our society today, leading to this spiritual longing being discarded or ignored, although offering clear residual evidence not only of its existence, but also of its prevalence in the human experience.

The second chapter builds an evidence-based framework for faith that is based in developmental psychology. It explores the evolution of spiritual consciousness as an essential aspect of basic human development, which occurs in tandem with evolutionary biology and developmental psychology. The chapter thus creates an intellectual bridge across three academic disciplines (biology, psychology, and theology) in making an empirical case for faith in a post-Christian world.

The second part of the book explores how faith is often messy and tumultuous. What has typically been valued in Christian spirituality is an unhealthy dependency on certainty that leaves little room for ambiguity. As a result, the church in the west is now facing a sprawling migrant crisis of its own making, with millions of spiritual refugees displaced somewhere between apostasy and heresy, and who find asylum by default in agnosticism. Most recently, some have called this sense of disillusionment, "deconstruction." John Bloom suggests that although the term deconstruction can mean many things in various contexts, it is a postmodern philosophy that has been adopted by many evangelical Christians to describe someone undergoing a faith crisis. Yet, to many Christians, "deconstruction also sometimes means pinpointing destructive cultural influences that warp the true gospel, to sometimes mean questioning and disallowing traditional evangelical doctrine and other symbols of authority, or to sometimes mean leaving the faith altogether."[4]

However, postmodern philosophy itself has been adapted from Jacques Derrida's life work, in which he calls our relationship to our conceptions of meaning "deconstruction." The *Stanford Encyclopedia of Philosophy* describes this model "as a set of critical, strategic and rhetorical practices employing concepts such as difference, repetition, the trace, the simulacrum, and hyperreality to destabilize other concepts such as identity, historical progress, epistemic certainty, and the univocity of meaning."[5] Thus, deconstruction, according to Bloom, is how "human language at best communicates, not absolute truth, but how a certain individual conceives of truth at a certain moment in time, in the contexts of his cultural, political, religious, environmental, and experiential influences."[6]

The third chapter highlights the need for a safe harbor for those who have been spiritually displaced. It deals with those who grew up in the church but are beginning to question the truth of Christianity. Feeling like renegades, many such people choose to live as expats in a self-imposed exile. The chapter thus issues an invitation to freely explore doubts and questions without repercussions, obligations, or judgment, and perhaps find a way back home again.

Chapter four explores how postmodernism is reshaping the world, and whether we are conscious of it or not, the world has changed, and it has changed forever. Thus, especially relevant to our discussion is how this new powerful cultural narrative is remaking the world as Christianity wanes; and how an embedded mistrust of institutions is remaking the church in an age when truth is relegated to individual tribes. How does the church function in an age where its story has become one of many and no longer central?

The third part of the book explores faith in practice, as it is within Christian orthodoxy, and deals directly with some of the primary objections people raise about the truth of Christianity. Subsequent chapters look at each objection in turn through four critical questions:

(1) *The Origin Question:* Did God create the world? Chapter five explores the creation of the universe from both biblical and scientific perspectives. Many within the broader culture today see the former as mythological and the latter as empirical. This chapter is especially important for those who view science and faith as adversaries rather than companions.

(2) *The Historicity Question:* Did Jesus of Nazareth really exist? Chapter six explores the existence of Jesus Christ from an ethnographical perspective. Can his existence be confirmed and triangulated apart from the biased biblical sources? Are there any contemporary historians who corroborate his existence in the historical documents of early antiquity?

(3) *The Veracity Question:* Are the gospels a reliable source? Anyone who has played telephone in elementary school knows that the message the teacher gives in the beginning is rarely the

same message when it reaches the end of the line. Usually, the original message has changed into something entirely different. How then could the message of Jesus still be the same here and now after two thousand years?

(4) *The Paranormal Question:* Does God still speak today? How can we be certain that it is God who is speaking and not just our imagination? How might we distinguish between a sign from God and mere coincidence?

My great hope for this book is twofold: first, that after weighing the evidence, seekers and skeptics reframe their notion of faith from a leap to something judicious—or at least not crazy. As Anne Lamott writes in *Traveling Mercies*, coming to faith may not be a leap but instead a series of staggers from what seemed like one safe place to another.[7] Second, it is my hope that readers who grew up in the church find confidence in the truth of the gospel, stirring their passion for God and his kingdom once again. Shall we begin? As we embark on our journey together, I give you the words Jesus gave to his disciples at the beginning of their journey: come and see!

REFLECTION QUESTIONS

1. As Anne Lamott writes in *Traveling Mercies,* coming to faith may not be a leap, but instead a series of staggers from what seemed like one safe place to another. How does that framework fit with the trajectory of your own faith journey?

2. Many view science as empirical and faith as mythological, yet it is nevertheless an empirical fact that ancient humans, as well as those who live in the modern world today, possessed or possess a lifelong longing for transcendence, meaning and purpose. Does that notion resonate with you?

3. Have you ever considered the idea that the rise of spiritual consciousness ("A Holy Haunting") is not merely a byproduct of cultural factors as many assume, but rather an echo resounding from eternity (as suggested) in this chapter?

4. What if the real problem is that we've been looking at faith all wrong? The rise of modernism was both a blessing and curse for the church. For while the modernists articulated belief in a rational and coherent fashion, they reduced its mystery and wonder. What if faith is at its core not a set of beliefs, but instead who we are in the deepest sense, i.e., beings forged in the corridors of eternity who predate the primordial universe and the Big Bang? Do you at times reduce faith to a set of beliefs?

A PRAYER

A Skeptic's Prayer:

God, I don't know whether you even exist. I'm a skeptic. I doubt. I think you may be only a myth. But I'm not certain (at least not when I'm completely honest with myself). So, if you do exist, and if you really did promise to reward all seekers, you must be hearing me now. So, I hereby declare myself a seeker, a seeker of the truth, whatever it is and wherever it is. I want to know the truth and live the truth. If you are the truth, please help me.[8]

Peter Kreeft and Ronald K. Tacelli

PART I:
FAITH IN THEORY

Chapter 1

A Holy Haunting

"The deep calls unto deep."
Psalm 42:7

Richard Dawkins, the Oxford evolutionary biologist and pugnacious atheist, infamously once had printed in bold on the cover of his book the notion that God is a delusion. In Dawkins' own words, faith, no matter how sincere or treasured, is a delusion. In *The God Delusion,* he mocks prayer, equating it with calling upon a sky fairy.[9] For many in the broader culture today, this polemical assertion simply rings true. Many believe faith is a leap into the dark armed with nothing but a whim. At best, faith is a placebo; at worst, it is a delusion.

By contrast, Francis Collins, director of the National Institute of Health—the largest and most prestigious biomedical research institution in the world—tells a radically different story.

He writes that based on previous research, "about 40 percent of biologists, physicists, and mathematicians purport to believe in a God who actively communicates with humankind and answers prayer."[10] Why then do Dawkins and those in the broader culture continue to denigrate faith as antithetical to science, when close to half of professional scientists believe unequivocally in the existence of a personal God?

Clearly, faith is deeply misunderstood, not only for such a mischaracterization to exist, but to account for the degree to which such a characterization now pervades the culture. What if the real problem is that we've been looking at faith all wrong? The rise of modernism was both a blessing and curse for the church, because while modernists articulated belief in a succinct and coherent fashion, they reduced the mystery and wonder of faith. What if faith is not at its core a set of beliefs, but is instead who we are in the deepest ontological sense, i.e., beings forged in the corridors of eternity predating the primordial universe and the big bang? What if the rise of spiritual consciousness is not a mere byproduct of cultural factors as many assume, but rather an echo resounding from eternity?

This chapter suggests a working framework to describe faith that is both biblically-grounded and evidence-based. This proposed framework defines faith as the expression of a lifelong evolutionary longing to make meaning of human existence in terms of a higher plane of reality. Although we've grown accustomed to the idea that growing physically and emotionally are indispensable to human flourishing, somewhere along the way in our post-Christian culture, we have excluded the dimension of spiritual growth.

We view science as empirical and faith as mythological, yet from an ethnographical perspective, it is an empirical fact that ancient humans, along with those who live in the modern world today, possessed or possess a lifelong longing for transcendence, meaning and purpose. Such longings fall under the purview of faith, but nonetheless permeate the human experience in a universal way.

Perhaps this is the very reason human beings have always longed to be part of something greater than themselves. Hence, faith in the deepest sense is primordial, because it connects the eternal with the present, unraveling the mystery of God's preeminence—which exists outside time and space—conflated and present in a precise moment in time.

St. Augustine of Hippo captures this poignant haunting that lurks in the deepest part of the human experience in his *Confessions*, when he writes: "You have made us for Yourself, O Lord, and our hearts are restless until they rest in You."[11] The very presence of God emanates from eternity. Faith is the echo and eternity is the origin.

FACING A SPIRITUAL VOID

In an op-ed in the *New York Times*, David Brooks notes our society is at this present moment facing a spiritual void. He suggests that we have "tried to medicalize trauma. We call it PTSD and regard it as an individual illness that can be treated with medication. But it's increasingly clear that trauma is a moral and spiritual issue as much as a psychological or chemical one."[12] Clearly, Brooks is pointing to a dimension of brokenness that physicians or therapists can't reconcile or resolve. As the current mental health crisis looms globally, our society and its most seasoned experts are at a loss. So many people today aren't feeling very well but aren't sure exactly why.

The psalmist writes in Psalm 42:7 that "deep calls unto deep." Many confuse this deep longing with a form of chronic anxiety, or something that has gone wrong, when it is in fact a holy haunting of the presence of God. Deep calling unto deep is nothing other than the voice of God echoing from eternity. David Brooks argues that the alarming increase in suicide and depression rates, along with the rise of fragility and distrust in our culture today, flow directly from this spiritual abyss. He writes, "when you privatize morality and denude the public square of spiritual content, you've robbed people of the community resources they need to process moral pain together."[13]

Clearly, the sacred and secular divide is proving problematic. Perhaps our culture's current crushing opioid crisis, mental health epidemic, and the rise of Tinder are all manifestations of this holy haunting gone horribly wrong—clear residual evidence of not only the existence of the sacred, but its prevalence in human experience. The need for the sacred to return to the center has never been clearer.

LONELINESS AS A SIGNPOST TO SOMETHING DEEPER

Woody Allen once joked that, "New York is just like everywhere else, except more so." New York does have more people, more restaurants, more diversity, and even more pigeons compared to most of the rest of the world. I grew up in uptown Manhattan right on Broadway, and take it from me, more doesn't always mean better. New York apartments are so tiny you feel like a sardine living in a can. This is good preparation for the daily commute, when you're squished into a metal cart twice a day. All New Yorkers know that proximity doesn't necessarily curate intimacy.

A recent national survey exploring the impact of loneliness revealed that this condition is now at epidemic levels in the United States and poses a severe health risk to the general population. Survey results were released by Cigna, a global health service company, based on the UCLA loneliness scale, an instrument that measures and assesses subjective feelings of loneliness, as well as social isolation, by using a 20-item questionnaire. Four significant patterns related to feelings of loneliness and social isolation emerged from the survey of more than 20,000 U.S. adults, aged eighteen years and older:

Nearly half of the respondents reported feeling alone occasionally or continuously, or left out. One in four rarely or never feel as if there are people who truly understand them. Two in five feel that their relationships are inconsequential and that they are isolated from others. One in five report they rarely or never feel close to other people or that there is anyone they can talk to.[14]

Bob Dylan once said that New York is the only place where you can freeze to death on a busy street, and no one will even notice.[15] Although urban centers are incredibly dense and swarming with people, the density only seems to compound the loneliness. Thus, the confluence of urbanization and globalization is inadvertently leading to feelings of loneliness and social isolation at unprecedented levels. What then does the debilitating impact of loneliness teach us about what it means to be human?

Solomon tells us in Ecclesiastes that God has placed eternity in our hearts. Loneliness peels back the curtain of a time long past. It shows us intuitively what quantum physics is now confirming: that at a subatomic level everything and everyone is interconnected. Darrell Johnson, a long-time Professor at Regent College in Vancouver, and one of Bono's favorite preachers,[16] was studying to become a theoretical physicist before he was seized by the beauty of God's transcendence. In *Experiencing the Trinity*, he writes:

> At the center of the universe is a relationship, that is the most fundamental truth I know. At the center of the universe is a community. It is out and for that relationship you and I were created and redeemed. It turns out that there is a three-fold-ness to that relationship. It turns out that the community is the trinity. The center of reality is Father, Son and Holy Spirit.[17]

What then does the debilitating impact of loneliness unveil about what it means to be really human and the deepest human longing? In short, loneliness is a signpost to something chasmic. At the deepest level, the human heart aches for relationships more than anything else. This is because God himself is a community within the fellowship of the Trinity. We desire to be in communion because before the advent of creation itself, God was part of an eternal fellowship. This ache in the human heart is clear residual evidence that we were created from community and for community.

No wonder so many people feel deeply alone and disconnected. If the residual imprint of the Trinity is lodged that deeply within our hearts, nothing will ever feel right until there is a homecoming of a sort. In *Four Quartets*, T. S. Eliot imagines existentially what such a homecoming might feel like. "We should not cease from exploration and at the end of all our exploring we will arrive at the place we started and know the place for the first time."[18] For if, as Darrell Johnson suggests, the center of the universe is a relationship and the center of reality is Father, Son, and Holy Spirit, then the center of our lives will ring hollow until this eternal community is front and center in our lives.

As part of NASA's Child Star program, a student asked NASA scientists a question so seemingly rudimentary that the assistance of a *"literal"* rocket scientist in answering it felt more than a little unnecessary. "What is gravity?" the student asked. Shockingly, the NASA scientists shrugged:

> NASA scientist 1: "We don't really know: We can define what it is as a field of influence because we know how it operates in the universe."
> NASA scientist 2: "Actually, some scientists think that it is made up of particles called gravitons which travel at the speed of light."
> NASA scientist 1: "However, if we are to be honest, we do not know what gravity 'is' in any fundamental way—we only know how it behaves."[19]

As Sir Isaac Newton discovered, gravity is a force of attraction that exists between any two masses, any two bodies, and any two particles. So too there exists a primal and intrinsic desire in the human heart to belong to a community. Although the struggle of loneliness itself is invisible to the naked eye, when we begin to explore the shocking distress that social isolation causes our basic biology at a fundamental level—we find that communal health and mental health are inextricably linked. At our core, the need to belong is what makes us human. It is as basic as our need for food and water, or at least that is what people realize when they've been deprived of such belonging.

Consequently, it appears that community is not a pleasant luxury, but a prerequisite for survival. For example, Dr. Douglas Nemecek, chief medical officer for behavioral health at Cigna notes, "loneliness has the same impact on mortality as smoking 15 cigarettes a day, making it even more dangerous than obesity."[20] As a result, social isolation is akin to a fish out of water gasping for oxygen. It turns out, we need community as much as we need air to breathe.

DEPRESSION AS A SIGNPOST TO SOMETHING HIGHER

Many have spoken about a collective dissatisfaction found in the human experience. C. S. Lewis once remarked, "If I find in myself a desire which no experience in this world can satisfy, the most probable explanation is that I was made for another world."[21] The infamous cultural icon Kanye West, in a track entitled "Runaway" on his Grammy-winning album *My Beautiful Dark Twisted Fantasy*, writes: "I always find, I always find. I always find, something wrong. I'm so gifted at finding what I don't like the most."[22] Yet, perhaps there is no one more cynical than Solomon—with his penchant for abusing the exclamation mark—writing in the book of Ecclesiastes, "'Meaningless! Meaningless!' says the Teacher. 'Utterly meaningless! What has been will be again, what has been done will be done again; there is nothing new under the sun. Everything is meaningless!'"

Although Solomon never binge-watched a show on Netflix, he already knew that feeling most of us get when the final credits roll in: that everything is meaningless—at least until we find something new to watch. If we've learned anything in the modern age, it is as Bruce Springsteen once poignantly sang, "Everybody has a hungry heart." Nothing in this world seems to satisfy. This collective dissatisfaction isn't just an ephemeral mid-life crisis in the human story. It stretches out for millennia. From the dawn of western civilization in ancient Mesopotamia to the big bright lights shining over Times Square in New York City, those words from C. S Lewis have resonated deeply. The truth is that we are still haunted by rumors of another world and still searching for something to fill our collective void.

Inexplicably, despite living at the pinnacle of human ingenuity and extravagance, many young people today are grappling with depression and thoughts of suicide. Epidemiologists, along with public health institutions, have tried to quantify the various factors driving the current mental health epidemic, but are only just beginning to scratch the surface. For example, two disturbing patterns discovered among young adults in the study of loneliness (Cigna) joined with the data on depression (Harvard), are that Gen Z is now the loneliest generation in history, as well as being the most at risk of suicidal ideation and self-harm.

A popular axiom is that "misery loves company." and based on the aggregate of those two groundbreaking quantitative studies on loneliness and depression, you could say that this aphorism is prophetic. For college students are not only battling loneliness as the Cigna study indicates, but also depression in tandem with suicidal ideation. If the loneliness epidemic belongs to a larger family of the current mental health crisis that is looming globally, then depression is a close relative. Misery does indeed seem to love company.

Published in *Depression and Anxiety*, the results of a study led by researchers at the Developmental Risk and Cultural Resilience Laboratory at Brigham and the Women's Hospital at Harvard Medical School reported on a survey of 68,000 college students from across more than 100 institutions for depression and suicidal ideation.[23] Four significant patterns emerged:

First, high rates of stressful life occurrences: 75 percent of respondents reported campus-related stress. Stress exposure was highly correlated with mental health issues, self-harm and suicidal ideation.

Second, ongoing mental health challenges: 25 percent of respondents reported seeking treatment or being diagnosed with some form of mental illness in the previous year. Twenty percent of all respondents struggled with suicidal ideation, with close to 10 percent reporting having attempted suicide and nearly 20 percent reporting self-injury.

Third, ethnic minorities are most at risk of hiding mental health struggles: Although the study revealed increased rates of stress, suicidal thoughts and attempts of self-harm, Asian and Black students reported a lower rate of mental health diagnoses compared to white students.[24]

Fourth, suicide rates among college students are double the national average: The study found one of five students surveyed reported thoughts of suicide in the last year.

The recent study on depression led by Harvard Catalyst together with Cigna's study on loneliness, shows an aggregating impact of stress and mental health struggles on college campuses.[25] The research tells of an ominous narrative looming in the hearts and souls of young adults in this generation, for it reveals students are not only battling enormous stress, but also depression and thoughts of suicide. Thus, countless young adults are not only feeling alone, but are grappling with an existential crisis so crippling they're desperately searching for reasons just to stay alive.

How can the most technologically connected generation be the most socially disconnected in human history? Moreover, how do we grapple with the incredible statistic that our most recently minted adults face a mortality rate higher than that of the Dark Ages?[26]

Daniel Groody, professor of theology at the University of Notre Dame, addresses this cultural conundrum: that the second leading cause of death among Gen-Z (18-22) is suicide, given that modern medicine has doubled our average life expectancy just in this century. He remarks:

> The paradox of our time in history is that we have more medicine but less wellness. We've been all the way to the moon and back, but have trouble crossing the street to meet a new neighbor. We conquered outer space but not inner space. We've done larger things but not better things. We've cleaned up the air but polluted the soul. We've conquered the atom but not our prejudice. We build more computers to hold

more information to produce more copies than ever, but we communicate less and less. These are the days of two incomes but more divorce, fancier houses but broken homes. These are the days of quick trips, disposable diapers, throwaway morality, one-night stands, and pills that do everything from cheer, to quiet, to kill. It is a time when there is much in the showroom window and nothing in the stockroom.[27]

As depression and anxiety reach epidemic levels and suicide rates skyrocket, the need for a return of the sacred to the center has never been clearer. This secular and sacred divide is obstructing our society's capacity to process our collective ailments, apart from the power of the liturgy. The holy sacraments, such as baptisms, weddings, and wakes, symbolize that our births, deaths, and those hallowed moments in between are sacred and not trivial. They are in fact gifts from above. The sacraments blow off the collective dust of our humdrum lives and give us a sacred purpose.

What then does the debilitating impact of depression among young adults today reveal about humanity's deepest longing? In short, depression is a signpost to something higher. The deepest part of us longs for a transcending purpose, because apart from such, our lives are devoid of dignity and inconsequential. It is no wonder so many young people today feel disheartened and hopeless; life apart from a sacred purpose life is meaningless.

The *Oxford Dictionary* defines haunting as something poignant and evocative; something difficult to ignore or forget. Brent Curtis and John Eldredge, who were professional counselors for many years, observed that a common thread that ran through most of their clients' lives was a poignant haunting; inviting them into a larger story than the one they were living; a life marked by a hallowed purpose, which they call a *Sacred Romance.*

> If we will listen, a sacred romance calls to us through our heart every moment of our lives. It whispers to us on the wind, invites us through the laughter of good friends, reaches out to us through the touch of someone we love. We've heard it in our favorite music, sensed it at the birth of our first child, been drawn to it while watching the shimmer of a sunset on the ocean. Romance is even present in times of great personal suffering: the illness of a child, the loss of a marriage, the death of a friend. Something calls to us through experiences like these and rouses an inconsolable longing deep within our heart, and the voice that calls to us in this place is none other than the voice of God.[28]

I know talk of religion today can often sound plastic and cliched, and not a genuine conversation. So, I will also make you a promise. I won't insult your intelligence and dress up a straw man only to swiftly knock him down simply to win an argument. My goal isn't to win religious arguments that you couldn't care less about, but rather to start a genuine dialogue about things that really matter and touch the deepest parts of our lives. The things we often ponder about in the middle of the night in those quiet unedited moments while fluffing our pillows, and when we are most unguarded and vulnerable. It is in those moments we feel a haunting that is quite hard to describe, but that is evocative and difficult to ignore.

SOMEWHERE BETWEEN KANSAS AND OZ

During her freshman year at Cornell, Rory was invited by a friend to attend a gathering on campus hosted by Intervarsity Christian Fellowship. As everyone lifted their voices and sang songs to God, she experienced a beauty and transcendence she had never felt before. She felt deeply affected by the gathering, because something so genuine about it touched almost every thread of her agnostic sense of life. At the same time, she also felt an immense discomfort, loneliness, and the poignant feeling that she didn't belong. Like Dorothy in the *Wizard of Oz*, she knew she wasn't in Kansas anymore, but the haunting was so overwhelming she decided to leave that semester and never returned. Yet, four years later, and somewhat to her surprise, Rory found herself sitting in the pews of a church in New York, out of place, still grappling, and still haunted by what she had experienced that one night in Ithaca.

Like the ionic song by the Beatles, the journey of faith is a "long and winding road" and not a straight path. Faith isn't monolithic or one-size-fits-all. It isn't linear, but is instead sinuous. Sometimes it gets worse before it gets better. God is a great artist and the Bible tells us he is painting a masterpiece and we are his canvas; except he isn't finished yet. Thus, we might not be able to connect the dots in our lives just yet, since dots often only make sense in reverse.

G. K. Chesterton writes in *Orthodoxy* that he had "always felt life first as a story: and if there is a story, there is a story-teller."[29] The truth is that our individual search for meaning points to a haunting in all of us that is almost primeval. It is simply instinctive for us to seek meaning outside ourselves, because we know for certain that we're living in a story we did not write.

I wrote this book to help you discover for yourself who the author of your story is and identify exactly where you are in that story. Many from my own dear faith community have found the house analogy very helpful in identifying where they might be in their faith. The house analogy starts with a simple question: Where are you with God today? Are you down God's block? At the front door or right inside the house? The house analogy helps those who are far, near, or somewhere in between determine their proximity to faith.

I also have a few suggestions on how to maximize the greatest value from this book based on your proximity to faith: far, near or somewhere in between. Here are my recommendations:

(1) *Far*: For those from secular and nonreligious backgrounds, making sense of life's ultimate meaning can be overwhelmingly lonely. Unlike the way it was for a young Luke Skywalker, who had Yoda to guide him, there is usually no such mentor. Well now there is. As I've mentioned already, this chapter and the next are aimed at bridging the divide between the secular and the sacred. To this end, I believe developmental psychology can help us incorporate an understanding of the evolution of spiritual consciousness as part of the natural progression of human development.

In addition, although all the chapters are important, chapters 5-8 deal directly with some of the primary objections raised against the historicity of Jesus and the truth of the Bible. Subsequent chapters focus on dismantling each objection in turn.

Furthermore, chapter five (on creation) is vital for those who view science and faith as adversaries rather than companions. Based on previous feedback from seekers within our own faith community, the single greatest barrier to faith is the notion that it is incompatible with science. The former is mythological, and the latter is empirical. This chapter attempts to bridge the divide.

(2) *Near*: If you are already a devoted believer, please consider reading this book together with those who are both far and others who are "somewhere in between" in their faith journey. All the chapters are important for building a case for faith in a post-Christian world, but chapter one (Holy Haunting) and chapter two (Spiritual Puberty) are especially relevant when it comes to the gap between the secular and the sacred.

(3) *Somewhere in Between*: For those of us who grew up in the church, questioning the truth of Christianity can feel like a betrayal. Chapter three (Spiritual Refugees) addresses how the church is facing a sprawling migrant crisis of its own making, with millions of spiritual refugees displaced somewhere between apostasy and heresy, who then find asylum by default in agnosticism.

In the age of deconstruction, most who begin struggling with their faith feel like renegades who are either a disappointment or a danger to the community, and as a result often choose to live as expats in a self-imposed exile. This chapter thus recognizes the pressing need for safe harbor for those who have been spiritually displaced, along with an invitation for fellow sojourners to freely explore doubts and questions without repercussions, obligations or any judgment, and perhaps find their way back home.

REFLECTION QUESTIONS

1. Where are you with God today? Are you down God's block? At the front door or right inside the house? (The house analogy helps those who are far, near, or somewhere in between determine their proximity to God.)

2. G. K. Chesterton writes in *Orthodoxy* that he had "always felt life first as a story: and if there is a story, there is a story-teller." The truth is that our individual search for meaning points to a haunting in all of us that is almost primeval. It is simply instinctive for us to seek meaning outside ourselves, because we know for certain that we're living in a story we did not write. How do *you* make sense of this lifelong haunting?

3. The confluence of urbanization and globalization is inadvertently leading to unprecedented loneliness and social isolation. What does the debilitating impact of loneliness teach us about what it means to be human?

4. The psalmist writes in Psalm 42:7 that "deep calls unto deep." Many confuse this deep longing with a form of chronic anxiety, or something that has gone wrong, when it is in fact a holy haunting of the presence of God. Deep calling unto deep is nothing other than the voice of God echoing from eternity. Do you think perhaps our culture's current crushing opioid crisis, mental health epidemic, and the rise of Tinder are all manifestations of this holy haunting gone horribly wrong?

PRAYER

You have searched me, LORD, and you know me. You know when I sit and when I rise; you perceive my thoughts from afar. You discern my going out and my lying down; you are familiar with all my ways. Before a word is on my tongue you, LORD, know it completely. You hem me in behind and before, and you lay your hand upon me.

Such knowledge is too wonderful for me, too lofty for me to attain. Where can I go from your Spirit? Where can I flee from your presence? If I go up to the heavens, you are there; if I make my bed in the depths, you are there.

If I rise on the wings of the dawn, if I settle on the far side of the sea, even there your hand will guide me, your right hand will hold me fast. If I say, "Surely the darkness will hide me and the light become night around me," even the darkness will not be dark to you; the night will shine like the day, for darkness is as light to you"

Psalm 139:1-12 (NIV)

Chapter 2
Spiritual Puberty

"My friend once told me that she loves her children much more than evolution requires."
David Brooks

THE EVOLUTION OF SPIRITUAL CONSCIOUSNESS

I mentioned earlier that I once believed girls were long-haired aliens from outer space. I also believed that *Nightmare on Elm Street* was a biopic about Freddie Krueger. I essentially became a caffeine-dependent insomniac in the middle of junior high, convinced that Freddie was going to murder me in my sleep. While my perception of reality might seem peculiar at first glance, if you sought out the opinion of a child psychologist, they would probably yawn in protest.

For children are instinctively more curious than they are well-behaved. In fact, you could argue that it is usually their curiosity that leads children into mischief and morality that constrains their curiosity. The former is instinctive, but the latter is instructive. Children must be taught to tell the truth but never to stretch it. If you think about it, it makes complete sense that children have egocentric projections about who they are, since they are often treated as if all revolves around them, and it usually does, although not for the reasons they might assume.

I once met a student at a New York medical school in Brooklyn who started his own religion. If it had not been Williamsburg, it probably wouldn't have been all that strange—I mean, that's where they invented skinny jeans for men and began retrofitting rustic factories for Tech start-ups. While the latter is pretty cool, I consider the former a mistake. I had been invited by a campus ministry to speak to about a hundred first-year med students who were exploring Christianity and afterwards, one of them approached me wanting to talk.

Initially, I thought he wanted to talk about my message, but soon realized he was more interested in having a conversation about starting his own religion. I told him that, like skinny jeans, no matter how he fashioned his religion, it would be incongruent with reality, but his appetite to make sense of the world was admirable. He called his new religion "Rayism"—yes, he had named it after himself. I guess it makes sense that someone studying to be a doctor might have a God complex and hence the potential to become a cult leader. Fortunately, he wasn't influential on campus and was his only member, which was relieving.

I expect one day Ray will look back on his time at medical school and laugh that he could believe in something so outlandish. In the meantime, he should probably avoid divulging that information during residency interviews, for we all know where hospitals put people who claim they've started their own religion. While it's true that Ray starting his own religion was both egocentric and idiosyncratic, such behavior is also typical of early childhood development. Robert Kegan, a child psychologist, suggests that children have a natural propensity to be "fantastic and illogical, their feelings impulsive and fluid, [and] their social-relating egocentric."[30]

Fantasy and imagination are characteristic of early childhood because that is when children first attempt to make sense of the world in light of their experience. In short, this projection in how we see the world and how we process what we see is what the *Merriam-Webster Dictionary* defines as consciousness. The dictionary offers two expansive definitions of "consciousness" that are especially relevant to this exploration of faith as a lifelong evolutionary longing, rather than merely the byproduct of cultural indoctrination or external influences.

Merriam-Webster defines consciousness as the quality or state of being aware, especially of something within oneself, and the state or fact of being conscious of an external object, state, or fact. Stephen Covey notes that it is "self-awareness that enables us to stand apart and examine even the way we 'see' ourselves—our self-paradigm, the most fundamental paradigm of effectiveness. It becomes our map of the basic nature of mankind."[31] Our capacity to differentiate ourselves from our environment is what makes us human. This conscious ability to distinguish between spatial objects, and between reality and fantasy is what separates us from all the other species living on our planet and is the primary catalyst for human ingenuity. As a result, from infancy to adolescence, we instinctively begin to develop a cognitive map to make meaning of life events, relationships, and ourselves.

Spiritual growth is in many ways like the tumultuous changes that occur during physical adolescence, except this time the change is taking place in the inner workings of the soul rather than the body. This is why I've coined this transformative process *Spiritual Puberty.* I have already discussed in the last chapter how, based on ethnographic research, spiritual hunger is just as, if not more primal than our need for food and sex, and when unmet has a negative impact on our individual and collective mental health.

Hence, this chapter presents an evidence-based framework for faith. Developmental psychology lays the groundwork for the evolution of spiritual consciousness as an essential part of basic human development, which works in tandem with evolutionary biology. In this way the chapter offers an intellectual bridge across the three academic disciplines of biology, psychology, and theology, and provides an empirical case for faith in a post-Christian world.

THE EVOLUTION OF CONSCIOUSNESS

The theory of the evolution of consciousness was developed by Robert Kegan, a renowned developmental psychologist at Harvard Graduate School of Education, who built on Jean Piaget's work on human intelligence among children. The heart of Kegan's theory of the evolution of consciousness articulates the "personal unfolding of ways of organizing experience that are not simply replaced as we grow but subsumed into more complex systems of mind."[32] This unfolding is a lifelong activity that commences in earliest infancy and progresses in complexity through a sequence of "evolutionary truces." Such truces are ways of resolving the tension between a longing for differentiation, and the equally poignant desire for inclusion and embeddedness between an organism and its environment (biology), and between the self and the other (psychology).[33]

In *The Evolving Self*, Kegan writes that, possessing both strengths and limitations, each evolutionary truce or balance is both an achievement of, and a constraint on meaning-making.[34] Each subsequent evolutionary truce is a new, more refined, solution to the lifelong tension between how people are connected, attached, and included and how people are simultaneously distinct, independent, and autonomous, differentiated from other people and the rest of the world. There is thus ongoing reconstruction of the relationship of persons and their environment.[35]

In short, Kegan explores critical ways of better understanding human life problems through a process he calls "meaning-making," the activity of making sense of experience by discovering and resolving problems. Each evolutionary truce or balance is achieved primarily through one's experience. Kegan writes, "it is not that a person makes meaning, as much as that the activity of being a person is the activity of meaning-making."[36] Kegan saw this developmental process of making sense of one's experience through discovering and resolving problems as the central activity of meaning making. All of this reminds me of a story involving my older brother and Newton's third law of motion.

In the third grade, and after watching Christopher Reeve in *Superman*, my brother broke both his legs by jumping off our roof wearing nothing but his underwear and a blanket as a cape. In so doing, he discovered firsthand the reality of Newtonian physics: for every reaction there is an equal and opposite reaction. In his initial descent his body was still in the air exerting a downward force to the concrete, which was itself exerting an equal upward force to his body, resulting in a violent collision and two broken legs. He thought he could fly until he discovered an invisible, yet unassailable force called gravity. This experience taught him to distinguish between fantasy and reality. He discovered that Christopher Reeves wasn't actually Superman, but merely playing such a character on television.

Although it can be devastating for a third-grade boy to discover he cannot fly, that discovery can also be a saving grace, especially if it saves him from an early death. Even to this day my brother has acrophobia, and all things considered, I don't think there's anything irrational about that if it keeps him off the roof. Experience can be a ruthless teacher. The lesson always comes after the test, but boy do we learn. My brother discovered an evolutionary truce lying immobile on his bed for months that he would never live down: the reality that he wasn't made for the sky, but for the ground. He realized the constraints of his own physiology and the consequences of living in the physical world.

Jean Piaget, a renowned Swiss epistemologist who created a unifying theory of human cognition with his seminal work about children, calls what my brother took away from his collision with gravity, "a schematic accommodation." According to Piaget, children inadvertently develop mental complexity from infancy, as they begin to develop a cognitive map to make meaning of life events, relationships, and themselves. This development occurs in four stages from infancy to adolescence:[37]

1. Sensorimotor: (0-2): Coordination of sense and abilities.
2. Preoperational (2-7): Rise of symbolic thought.
3. Concrete: (7-11): Development of mental operations.
4. Formal: (11-on): Developmental ability to think both abstractly and logically.

Kegan, who prized "building strong intellectual bridges" across disciplines, believed he could create a more holistic theory of human development by integrating Jean Piaget's work on human intelligence in children with his own work. The two critical evolutionary tensions that Kegan explores and integrates into his theory in the evolution of consciousness are:

1. The tension between the organism and the environment (developed in biological terms by Piaget).
2. The tension between self and other (developed in psychological terms by Kegan).

Kegan builds on Jean Piaget's seminal work on human intelligence among children and reconciles the first evolutionary longing that exists between organisms and the environment. First and foremost, Piaget saw human development solely in biological terms, as nothing more than complex living organisms that must evolve to survive the environment in which they are embedded. For Piaget, the business of evolution is the same in "protozoa, coleus plants, and elephants as it is [for] human beings."[38]

In short, all living organisms aim on a molecular level to prolong their lives. This is why my dog instinctively follows me into the kitchen, constantly on the lookout for food, or why sometimes that fly on the wall seems impossible to kill; and even why there is a post-humanist dream of downloading human consciousness into a digital medium to escape death and achieve immortality. Intuitively, life prioritizes life. Kegan notes that "Piaget's principal loyalty was to the ongoing conversation between the individuating organism and the world" in which it is embedded.[39]

Kegan often notes that Piaget's genius in the field of human cognition was the inspiration for his own work, for it helped him better understand the developmental processes of children.[40] However, Kegan also believed that Piaget neglected the emotional aspects in children that are often embedded in the developmental process. He thus sought to fill that gap, noting that the one main factor that drove his research was the wish to aid all professionals who concern themselves with growth and development, so as to build greater empathy between psychotherapists, counselors, teachers, and pastors.[41] Kegan writes:

> That "energy field" which to the evolutionary biologist may be about "adaptation," is as much as anything about the very exercises of hope. Were we "all limit" (all "assimilation"), there would be no hope; "all possibility" (all "accommodation"), no need of it. Might we better understand others in their predicament if we could somehow know how their way of living reflects the state of their hoping at this

depth?—not the hopes they have or the hoping they
do, but the hopes and hoping they are? [42]

Just as Kegan was inspired by Piaget's genius, I am stirred
by Kegan's brilliance in creating viable maps of the evolution
of human consciousness related to basic human development.
And by the same token, I also see Kegan's instinct as a psychologist leading him to neglect the spiritual dimension in the
critical unfolding of human development. As a theologian and
minister, I also seek to fill in the gaps I have sensed Kegan may
have overlooked.

TOWARDS A MORE HOLISTIC MAP OF HUMAN DEVELOPMENT

First, in *Over Our Heads,* written in 1994, Kegan addresses the
taxing mental demands of modern life. The ever-increasing and
growing complexity of modern life creates a baffling array of
expectations, prescriptions, claims, and demands on the way
we know the world, ourselves, and others, and the way we are
expected to understand it. In short, Kegan argues that if our
inner lives cannot keep pace with the complexity and often confounding claims modern life makes, we will feel, as we often
do, in over our heads. Yet his notion of expanding mental complexity as an open-ended process, born of the dynamic inter-
action between meeting cultural demands and emerging mental
capabilities, doesn't feel quite sufficient to match all the growing demands of modern life. This is because the problems we
often face are not always emotional or biological; they are also
at times spiritual. Just as there are different maps for the mind
and body that are mutually exclusive—and this is why they have

branched out in their respective disciplines—a theological map navigates through the complexity of spiritual tensions, just as medicine and psychology navigate through the contours of body and mind. Theology came before the other two, I might add, but is now deemed a tertiary and anecdotal way of seeing the world. But could the modern world have thrown the baby out with the bathwater too soon?

Second, if Kegan thought modern life was complex and confounding in 1994, do we have any hope of navigating through the ever-growing multiplicity of a postmodern world today? Kegan's world in 1994 predates the advent of Windows 95, Dell, and the revolution of personal computing. People were using cassette players rather than iPods. This was a world without the iPhone, Google and social media. Social media alone has brought with it crushing new expectations which an earlier world could never have conceived. Every loss and win is compounded with greater anxiety and paranoia. And when we compare other people's fastidiously curated highlights to our own bloopers, despair is inevitable.

No wonder so many young adults today have a tendency to remove themselves from community and into social isolation. It is no surprise that Generation Z (aged 18–22) is now the loneliest generation in history. Although Gen Z is perhaps the generation that is most technologically connected, they scored the highest on the UCLA loneliness scale. Tragically, many young adults are looking for any sort of reprieve from the crushing expectations they and their peers have for themselves. This is a significant discovery, for it reveals that perhaps there has never been a generation more starved of love than that of today's young adults.

Many believe their lives aren't good enough. It seems ironic for a generation that is supposedly "adulting" to be struggling with perfectionism, but when your life is under constant scrutiny, this becomes almost inescapable.

Thus, Kegan's solution of narrowing the gap between the complex demands of modern life and our own mental capacities helps, but isn't enough. As the current mental health crisis looms globally, our society and its most seasoned experts are at a loss. So many people today aren't feeling very well, but aren't sure exactly why. Both physicians and economists have tried to quantify the various factors driving the current mental health epidemic, but are also lost. Although we have conducted thousands of quantitative and qualitative studies in academic medicine around the themes related to mental health, we really are only just beginning to scratch the surface.

As mentioned earlier, in his *New York Times* op-ed, David Brooks writes about how "our society has tried to medicalize trauma. We call it PTSD and regard it as an individual illness that can be treated with medication. But it's increasingly clear that trauma is a moral and spiritual issue as much as a psychological or chemical one."[43] Clearly, Brooks is pointing to a degree of brokenness that physicians or therapists can't reconcile or resolve.

Thus, what we need is an entirely new map to help us identify and negotiate these confounding problems in modern life, a more holistic map of the evolution of consciousness that converges on the spirit (theology) in tandem with the body (biology) and the soul (psychology). The divide between the sacred and secular has not only created a spiritual void, but somewhere along the way, it has also become accepted in the post-Christian world that while developing physically and emotionally is essential for basic human development (a notion Piaget and Kegan both helped popularize), there is no need for a spiritual center.

In response to this spiritual void (or tension) that is affecting our culture today, I propose a third evolutionary truce, one that is absent from the developmental literature and from Kegan's seminal work. This novel addition resolves the tensions between the longing for differentiation and the equally poignant desire for inclusion and embeddedness between creation and creator. Many view faith as anecdotal, yet from an ethnographical perspective, it is an empirical fact that ancient humans, along with those who live in the modern world today, possessed or possess a lifelong longing for transcendence, meaning and purpose.

If our evolution as a species is limited only to the biological and psychological aspects of human development, then why do we continue to ask questions that move beyond where we live and with whom; questions that attempt to make sense of human existence on a higher plane of reality, such as life origins and the formation of the primordial universe; and questions that move beyond the temporal to the eternal? St. Augustine of Hippo captures this confounding haunting that lurks in the deepest part of the human experience in his *Confessions*, when he writes: "A human being as such is a huge abyss. It is easier to count his hairs than his moods or the workings of his heart."[44]

The Apostle Paul, addressing this tension that exists between creation and its creator, writes, "The whole creation has been groaning as in the pains of childbirth right up to the present time." For the creation was subjected to frustration, not by its own choice, but by the will of the one who subjected it, in hopes that the creation itself will be liberated from its bondage to decay and brought into the freedom and glory of the children of God (Rom. 8:20-22, NIV).

Thus, a revised theory of the evolution of human consciousness now presents three evolutionary truces that parallel the three evolutionary tensions in the critical unfolding of the model of basic human development:

1. *Between the organism and environment (explored by Piaget in biological terms).*
2. *Between the self and other (explored by Kegan in psychological terms).*
3. *Between creation and creator (explored in spiritual terms in chapter 1 as a "Holy Haunting," with the critical unfolding of this process described as "spiritual puberty").*

This addition of a spiritual aspect to the model of basic human development offers a more holistic understanding, one that is grounded in the best ethnographic research and developmental psychology. In addition, this model not only better reflects the totality of the human experience, but also helps build an intellectual bridge across multiple academic disciplines; it bridges the secular and sacred divide; it eliminates old hostilities; and it fosters greater collaboration between science and faith.

SCIENCE AND FAITH AS COMPANIONS

All the branches of science, but especially the social sciences, answer questions of "how." Theology answers "why." Psychology can expound on how the cognitive developmental process in children works or how the orders of consciousness related to the evolution of meaning unfold, but it cannot tell you why it does; just that it does. Empirical research is limited to exploring plausible correlations of a phenomenon of interest, and does not cover causation. Reaching generality is never the goal; pushing the boundaries of human knowledge is, but only within a dimension that is measurable. Hence, when it comes to answering life's ultimate questions, such as why we're here in the first place, or why we seek to make meaning at all, science is silent. This is not because science is opposed to faith, but because science has no parameters for such inquiry; and it is important to recognize the difference. This growing polarization between faith and science is something I will unpack in greater detail in chapter five.

In *A Brief History of Time,* speaking of possibly discovering an eloquent and unified theory of everything, Stephen Hawking writes, "Then we shall all, philosophers, scientists, and just ordinary people, be able to take part in the discussion of the question of why it is that we and the universe exist. If we find the answer to that, it would be the ultimate triumph of human reason—for then we would know the mind of God."[45] Although I am not certain when such a theory will emerge even as we push the boundaries of human knowledge, I do not believe we have to wait eons to touch the mind of God. We can see beyond the horizon through faith. The scope and framework of our inquiry doesn't have to be limited to our fancied binaries.

Although I have my own preferences, I use both Apple and Microsoft applications, based on what is needed in the moment. In fact, right now I am on my beautiful MacBook Air using Microsoft's Word to write this book! Clearly, tools were meant to be utilized, not politicized. The point is, we can utilize multiple maps to explore the world. This inquiry doesn't have to be limited to an AND/OR paradigm. It can be BOTH/AND. Compared to the vastness of the universe, our epistemological differences are inconsequential, and our only loyalty should be to pushing the boundaries of human knowledge further than before.

Addressing the relationship between faith and reason, Augustine of Hippo once said, *Credo ut intelligam,* which is Latin for "I believe so that I may understand."[46] In short, faith is not lack of reason, but is the aptitude to see beyond it. There are multiple maps to discovery; there need not be polarity in our exploration. In fact, Kegan wrote that what inadvertently led him to the field of developmental psychology was an initial hunger drawing him to literature, philosophy and theology.[47] Multiple disciplines can complement one other in our discussion of life's ultimate questions.

ECHOES OF ETERNITY

My wife recently found five eastern tiger swallowtail butterfly larvae on an aromatic dill plant in the back of our home garden. She decided to adopt them because she learned that these beautiful creatures rarely become full grown butterflies due to turbulent environmental factors and the threat of predators. So she brought them into the house, and we hosted them in the habitat of our former hermit crab that died a few years ago. (I know he is looking down from hermit heaven, caring for our visitors, RIP little guy.) As we watched the larvae transform into caterpillars, we realized for the first time just how much nurture the process of metamorphosis actually requires. No wonder only one out of ten survive! We gave them the dill my wife was growing in our garden as their host plant and fed them tons of parsley, barely keeping pace with their insatiable appetites. At one point, some of those caterpillars got so plump, I thought about putting them into Weight Watchers.

Then one day the caterpillars stopped eating and started hanging themselves upside down on the glass of the habitat and spinning themselves into silky cocoons, which would then molt into lustrous chrysalises. We thought maybe a few had died because they didn't budge at all for a few days, but to our surprise, after a week or so, we saw beautiful wings begin to sprout inside the cocoons—and that is exactly how it feels sometimes in the darkest moments of our lives. It can feel as if our faith has died, and all meaning is lost; or maybe that we are just inconsequential blobs drifting aimlessly in empty space. Donald Miller in *A Million Miles in a Thousand Years* poignantly grapples with the tension between randomness and the beauty of purpose when he writes:

> Sometimes I'm tempted to believe life doesn't mean anything at all. I've read philosophers who say meaningful experiences are purely subjective, and I understand why they believe that, because you can't prove life and love and death are anything more than random happenings. But then you start thinking

about some of the scenes you've lived, and if you've had a couple of drinks, they have a sentimental quality that gets you believing we are all poems coming out of the mud.[48]

C. S. Lewis writes in *Mere Christianity* that "atheism turns out to be too simple. If the whole universe has no meaning, we should never have found out that it has no meaning: just as, if there were no light in the universe and therefore no creatures with eyes, we should never know it was dark. Dark would be a word without meaning."[49]

Yet sometimes the laws of nature paint a very different picture of the universe that we live in. When you see the lustrous chrysalis shed its cocoon and begin to pump its wings before it takes flight: your heart flutters with hope. I will always remember the day we released the butterflies from the safety of the habitat back into the garden. As the tiger swallowtail fluttered its wings and danced between the hydrangeas, marigolds, and roses, it felt as if we stole a brief glimpse into Eden before the fall; and it is in that moment I believed that, just maybe, we are all poems coming out of the mud.

REFLECTION QUESTIONS

1. If our evolution as a species is limited only to our biological and psychological aspects, then why do we continue to ask questions that move beyond where we live and with whom, questions that attempt to make sense of human existence on a higher plane of reality? Why do we contemplate the origins of life and the formation of the primordial universe and ask questions that move beyond the temporal to the eternal?

2. In many ways, spiritual growth is like the tumultuous changes that occur during physical adolescence, only this time the change is taking place in the inner workings of the soul rather than the body. This is why I've coined this transformative process *spiritual puberty.* I discussed in the last chapter ways in which spiritual hunger is just as, if not more primal than our need for food and sex, and if unmet has a negative impact on our individual and collective mental health. Can you relate?

3. C. S. Lewis writes in *Mere Christianity* that "atheism turns out to be too simple. If the whole universe has no meaning, we would never have found out that it has no meaning: just as, if there were no light in the universe and therefore no creatures with eyes, we should never know it was dark. Dark would be a word without meaning." What then does this lifelong longing for meaning, purpose and transcendence reveal about who we are in the deepest sense?

4. Donald Miller in *A Million Miles in a Thousand Years* poignantly grapples with the tension between randomness and the beauty of purpose when he writes:

"Sometimes I'm tempted to believe life doesn't mean anything at all. I've read philosophers who say meaningful experiences are purely subjective, and I understand why they believe that, because you can't prove life and love and death are anything more than random happenings. But then you start thinking about some of the scenes you've lived, and if you've had a couple of drinks, they have a sentimental quality that gets you believing we are all poems coming out of the mud."

Does that strike you as a scene you may have lived before?

A PRAYER

For the creation waits in eager expectation for the children of God to be revealed. For the creation was subjected to frustration, not by its own choice, but by the will of the one who subjected it, in hope that the creation itself will be liberated from its bondage to decay and brought into the freedom and glory of the children of God.

We know that the whole creation has been groaning as in the pains of childbirth right up to the present time. Not only so, but we ourselves, who have the first fruits of the Spirit, groan inwardly as we wait eagerly for our adoption to sonship, the redemption of our bodies. For in this hope we were saved. But hope that is seen is no hope at all. Who hopes for what they already have? But if we hope for what we do not yet have, we wait for it patiently.

In the same way, the Spirit helps us in our weakness. We do not know what we ought to pray for, but the Spirit himself intercedes for us through wordless groans. And he who searches our hearts knows the mind of the Spirit, because the Spirit intercedes for God's people in accordance with the will of God.

Romans 8:20-27 (NIV)

PART II:
FAITH IN PROCESS

Chapter 3
Spiritual Refugees

*"Even though I walk through the valley of the shadow
of death, I will fear no evil, for you are with me;
your rod and your staff, they comfort me."*
Psalm 23:4 (NIV)

WHEN THE RUG IS PULLED OUT FROM UNDER YOU

In the middle of the night, I received a frantic phone call from my dad. My mom had suffered a stroke just a few hours earlier. "Her situation is dire," my dad said, his voice quivering. I felt a chill go down my spine as the vibrations from his voice traveled from his lips to my ears. Hearing the usual buoyancy in my dad's voice replaced with a whimper, I calculated the chances of seeing my mom again alive were faint.

Until that moment, I had never once contemplated a life without my mother, nor had I ever had to. Although she stood barely five foot tall, her brazen ferocity and unassailable determination made her seem almost invincible. If anyone could escape the jaws of death, she could. This wasn't her first brush with death, nor would it be her last, for her resilience always prevailed. After all, she had survived the Korean War; a war with her wicked stepmother; and even a run-in with a Siberian tiger in the mountains of South Korea from which she had escaped unscathed.

I fell to the ground sobbing as I hung up the phone. After weeping hysterically for what seemed like an eternity, I only became aware of the river of tears and mucus streaming down my face when it reached the floor in my dorm room and formed a pool. I didn't know it then, but that pool of tears initiated a tsunami of doubt that would rip the seams off my youthful faith. The truth is, until that very moment, neither my life nor my faith had truly been tested, but when the test came, boy did it teach me something.

Homer writes in the *Odyssey* that a giant wooden horse, masquerading as a gift, entered the gates of Troy only to bring about the demise of the city. That is exactly how doubt found entry into my own heart. Just when I thought I finally found some solace in the hope of seeing my mother in heaven, and found my footing again, an insidious question pulled the rug out from under my feet. "What if heaven isn't real?" I dared to ask. The more I questioned, the more unsure I became, and the further I sank into despair. Before I knew it, in a blink of an eye, I was plunged into spiritual crisis. My own deconstruction had begun.

TO DOUBT IS HUMAN

Dr. Timothy Keller, the New York Times bestselling author of *The Reason for God*, describes a similar experience while grappling with his own impending death. After being diagnosed with stage four pancreatic cancer, and having spent a lifetime counseling others before his diagnosis, he wondered if he'd be able to take his own advice. In a poignant piece for the *Atlantic*, he wrote:

> For the same reason, our beliefs about God and an afterlife, if we have them, are often abstractions as well. If we don't accept the reality of death, we don't need these beliefs to be anything other than mental assents. But as death, the last enemy, became real to my heart, I realized that my beliefs would have to become just as real to my heart, or I wouldn't be able to get through the day. Theoretical ideas about God's love and the future resurrection had to become life-gripping truths or be discarded as useless.[50]

Tish Warren in *Prayer in the Night* describes experiencing the death of her unborn son in the emergency room while soaked in blood—her second miscarriage. She writes, "during that long year, as autumn brought darkening days and frost settled in, I was a priest who couldn't pray. I didn't know how to approach God anymore. There were too many things to say, too many questions without answers. My depth of pain overshadowed my ability with words. And, more painfully, I couldn't pray because I wasn't sure how to trust God."[51]

Yet, with hindsight, I've learned that struggling with doubt while grappling with loss is not apostasy; it is just human. It is only human to doubt everything you thought you once knew when your whole world comes crashing down. Imminent death has an uncanny ability to quickly cut through the hidden she-nanigans beneath the veneer of our faith and expose the utter frailty of our beliefs. This was certainly true of me upon hearing the news of my mother's brush with death. I wish someone had told me at the start of my own struggle with faith in college that it is human to doubt, and that doubt feels a lot like fear. You can't help but wonder if there is something wrong with you or with the world, or if the world is changing, or if you are. Change is supposed to feel like something is off, because something is.

Nonetheless, for those of us who grew up in the church, questioning the veracity of Christianity can feel almost like a betrayal. Feeling like renegades, many of us choose to live as vagabonds riddled with shame in a self-imposed exile. As a result, the church is now facing a sprawling migrant crisis of its own making, with millions of spiritual refugees displaced somewhere between faith and doubt, who find asylum by default only in agnosticism, because somehow we come to believe faith is opposed to doubt and not actually part of the process.

FAITH ISN'T OPPOSED TO DOUBT

My mother did end up surviving her brush with death, as did my faith. The experience did make me examine painstakingly why I believe what I believe, however. Yet my struggle wasn't over questions of theodicy. I wasn't grappling with why God allowed such calamity to befall my mother and my family. My struggle was much more insidious than doubts about God's character: I was questioning if God existed at all. My faith wasn't shaken because I felt that God hid his face, but rather that he may be an abstraction stemming primarily from my own neurosis.

I often wondered during those many sleepless nights if faith really were just a leap into the dark prompted by nothing but a whim, or if it truly points to the center of reality. If faith was a placebo at best and a delusion at worst, then it was time to walk away. Either Christianity was true, or it wasn't. It had eternal significance, or was inconsequential—there was nothing in between. My mother's looming death also forced me to abandon the many niceties and cliches surrounding religious belief, and pursue truth for truth's sake and follow it wherever it may lead.

One thing I realized while navigating the darkest spiritual crisis I had ever known, was that the church doesn't deal well with struggles marked by ambiguity. Ironically, unless your struggles are distinct and explicit you can be almost certain there isn't a ministry for them. A Celebrate Recovery program may exist for those struggling with various addictions, or there may be an Alcoholics Anonymous for recovering alcoholics, but there is no Agnostics Anonymous. There isn't a program where someone keeps you accountable for the last bout of doubt you had, nor is there a safe place to process those doubts. In short, structurally and systemically, the church today operates as if it were still back in the 1950s and sees the world only in black and white, whereas real life is fluorescent and lived in color.

Consequently, I also felt the most alone I've ever felt. I self-isolated and self-quarantined, riddled with shame because that seemed the only option available. In hindsight, I realize now that a church without a safe harbor is not only a church in danger, but a dangerous church. This speaks of the height from which we have fallen. Although the disciples had similar doubts, they never once had to go through them alone. If they doubted, they doubted together. For the early church, community and faith were inseparable; it would have been inconceivable to live them apart. The gospel writers clearly did not see doubt possessing the stigma we do today, because if they did, they would have deliberately chosen to omit such thoughts from the record rather than highlight them. No, they saw doubt as a genuine part of the human experience and as a prerequisite to developing authentic faith.

In the morning of the resurrection, a group of women who had encountered Jesus on the road after visiting his tomb kept shouting to his disciples, "He has risen!" However, although the disciples heard those exact words multiple times, they didn't really register. At least not then. Peter mumbled those same words back to the women in disbelief, for he couldn't find it in himself to believe them no matter how many times he said them. In protest, his heart could only utter one word: impossible! Afterwards, Peter brazenly tells the group of women who bore witness to the resurrection to stop talking nonsense, which translates today as "please shut up" with some expletives in between. The story of Easter did not begin with robust faith, but instead with incessant doubt. Thus, wherever you might be in your journey—whether full of faith or full of doubt or even somewhere in between—Easter is your story too. The story of Christianity begins with doubt, not belief.

We often forget this: that Christianity was born out of skepticism rather than belief. The disciples themselves clearly document in the gospels how they were teetering between fear and skepticism for much of their journey with Jesus, culminating in an epic collapse of faith on the morning of the resurrection! Clearly, faith isn't opposed to doubt; it is actually part of the process. In fact, you could go so far as to say that faith apart from doubt isn't faith at all. Faith is born out of the crucible of doubt.

As a side note to those who might be struggling with questions or doubts about the validity of the Christian faith, I deal directly with some of the primary objections people raise about the truth of Christianity from chapters five to eight. Subsequent chapters look at each objection in turn and examine them rigorously, one by one.

THE STING OF DISQUALIFICATION

Recently, two students attending Columbia University and wrestling deeply with their faith, asked individually if we could set up a zoom meeting to sort out a few things. Dylan is from Houston and Joel is from Singapore and they both grew up in the church. When I met with Dylan, I could tell he was deeply torn about something. He said that he wasn't yet quite sure, but probably wasn't a Christian anymore, and didn't know how to tell his parents. The very thought of breaking it to his parents was eating away at him more and more each day. Dylan's unbosoming, which was filled with many contradictions, told me everything and more about the burden he was carrying.

Joel had an entirely different worry. He had been the president of his church youth group before moving to Manhattan for school and just could not bear to share his doubts and numerous philosophical objections with his community back home because he was afraid of being a stumbling block to his friends.

Dylan and Joel's stories are too common. Most who begin struggling with their faith in the church feel like renegades who are either a disappointment or a danger to the community, and as a result, often choose to live as expats in a self-imposed exile.

A recent Gallup poll suggests this unraveling is already at work in the next generation. When asked about their denominational affiliation, the majority responded, "none." "None" is how the majority of Americans now identify their religious or spiritual affiliation.[52] A generation ago people inherited faith from their parents. If parents were Presbyterian, then the children were Presbyterian. But the "nones" are leaving behind an inherited faith and looking for spirituality away from the church. This group of "nones" is in transition. They are sojourners looking for home.

I've often heard about the dangers of young Christians losing their faith in college but didn't think it applied to me because I really believed that I was the exception. I thought to myself, What? No! This can't be. That happens to others, but not me. Like Peter, who brazenly told Jesus that he was willing to die for him only to deny him publicly thrice, I, too, soon realized that this delusion was also the operating principle from which I had lived out my life till then. The dark side of believing you're an exception, however, is what follows when you fail. One of the most difficult aspects of failing to live up to your own expectations is navigating through the inner shame that gnaws away incessantly.

Another important layer of the deconstruction of faith is identifying the harmful personal and cultural influences that distort the truth of the gospel. It was with incredulity that I realized

I was struggling to forgive myself even though God had already done so. In theory I was a Christian saved by God's grace, but in practice I was a humanist disguised as a Christian, spurning grace and struggling to save myself. This point introduces another aspect of salvation: we not only need to be saved from our doubts and fragility, but also from an agonizing feeling of disqualification that often follows when we fail to live up to our own expectations.

On a number of occasions, Jesus found his disciples essentially arguing amongst themselves about who they believed to be the G-O-A-T (the Greatest of All Time) in God's kingdom. The G-O-A-T debate continues to dominate the airwaves of all major sport networks without pause or delay. Anecdotally, for the last two millennia Christians have also debated who they believe is the Greatest Christian of all time. Many say the Apostle Paul, who is responsible for writing almost half of the New Testament, while many others have argued for Billy Graham, who preached the gospel to more people alive and online than anyone else in history.

Yet, we often forget that the G-O-A-T debate was already settled by Jesus once and for all and for all time. Jesus on one occasion brazenly looked into the crowd and declared that John the Baptist was the G-O-A-T of all G-O-A-Ts, knowing full well that in his darkest hour—the one who once bore witness through the power of the Holy Spirit that Jesus was the Messiah—would come to doubt him after being imprisoned and thrown into the darkness by King Herod. Yet Jesus still contended that John is not only the greatest prophet of all time, but also the greatest human ever to be born of woman! Hence, if the greatest prophet of all time doubted Jesus, then how much more will we? And if Jesus didn't disqualify John for his greatest misstep, then how much more will he forgive us in our darkest hours? This might sound ludicrous, but sometimes I wonder if we expect more from ourselves than God does. I know I have and often still do, but now I know that the gospel is good news because God doesn't call the qualified; he qualifies the called.

BECOMING A SAFE HARBOR

The Bible clearly teaches us that God's power is made perfect in our weakness and not our strength (see 2 Cor. 12:9). Ironically, this seems to go against not only our natural inclinations, but those of our churches as well. However, not only is this reaction unhealthy, but it is also far removed from reality. Life is full of opacity and messiness. It is naive to believe you can divorce one from the other. What has been typically valued in Christian spirituality is an unhealthy dependency on certainty that leaves little room for ambiguity when both life and faith are often messy and tumultuous.

The good news of the gospel is that Jesus came for those who are sick, sinful, and broken, not those who are healthy, moral, or whole. The latter creates a culture of isolation, deception, and manipulation, but the former emancipates us from chronic perfectionism and liberates us to live in authentic community, truth, and sincere love. The late Henri Nouwen once wrote: "As long as we continue to live as if we are what we do, what we have, and what other people think about us, we will remain filled with judgments, opinions, evaluations, and condemnations. We will remain addicted to putting people and things in their right place."[53] We must remember that the church is called to be an ER for the sick, and not a fashion show for the moral elite.

Once when Jesus was preaching to a crowd in his hometown in Galilee, he invited all those who were weary of their burdensome lives to come to him and find rest (Matt. 11:28-30). What was Jesus really saying? In short, come to me and fall apart. The invitation of the gospel is a promise of safe harbor for all who are barely holding on and ripping at the seams. Come. To. Me. And. Fall. Apart. But how exactly? And where can we unbosom our brokenness that is actually safe?

First, let's work to confess our struggles to one another rather than trying to hide them. This is not only healthy, but also foundational in creating a culture of grace. *How difficult is it for us to sincerely confess our struggles to others?* Yes, it will hurt our pride, but that is exactly why we should do it. It will bring light into the darkness, and with it, healing and restoration into our lives and others. Some call this renewal or transformation; others call it something else. Whatever the etymology, it is a God thing and that is always good.

Second, beggars can't be choosers, but it would seem we have too many of us who are pretending to be ok when we're clearly not. When we boldly boast in our weaknesses, we eliminate any ambiguity about who the actual hero is in our story. Yes, this is easier said than done, but the truth is humility never once felt good to me or anyone else. Humility is in fact poisonous to our pride and lust for control, but it is also the very place where God's grace begins to take its stride.

This was Tuna's story too. (Yes, that's the pseudonym she chose.) She left the church twice before returning because she encountered a church culture of rigidity, rules, and shame in her adolescence. Then, in college, she experienced a Christian community of half-baked truths, cookie cutter answers and chronic perfectionism. Shortly after, she interned at NASA Space Grant Consortium, then moved to NYC after graduating from Cornell to work as an engineer at American Express. This is when she found our community at 180 Church, and I had the awesome privilege of baptizing her into God's family last year.

Yet Tuna's gospel homecoming is a quintessential coming of age story about a life and faith in process that might not have been if some of the young women in our church had not countered her previous Stepford church experiences and instead modeled a culture of vulnerability and brokenness and openly shared their own struggles.

This, in turn, gave Tuna the courage to face and share her own broken story: her parent's divorce, her father's recent passing and her own inner brokenness—about who she really was; about what, and whom she had lost; about what she struggled with and was afraid of; about her mistakes and shame; and about how much she needed God. Tuna's poignant story shows us faith isn't always linear but is instead sinuous. Sometimes it gets worse before it gets better. Humility feels poisonous, but it is often the very place where God's grace begins to take stride. The following is an excerpt from her poignant testimony on the day of her baptism:

> Over the years, I've heard a lot of people talk about their big moment of coming to Christ, and even now I sometimes feel envious and wish I had some grand, obvious moment that changed my life in grand, obvious ways. In reality, every morning I have to make the grueling, deliberate choice to surrender to God once

more, and every change God has made in my life has taken a lot of time and struggle. But, like we all sang at a retreat couple of years ago, "the hills are alive with the sound of music." And now that I've heard the sound of music coming from the top of the mountain, I know I never want to stop climbing towards it.

Jesus said on one occasion that we must be born again spiritually to enter the kingdom of heaven, and on another, that we must become like little children. If the conception of faith can be compared to birth and puberty, then salvation is always going to be something of a mess.

I wish I'd known sooner. The famed psalm my mother recited nearly every day at dawn is true after all. You see, I once believed that I had to walk through the valley of the shadow of death alone. I thought that was how apostasy worked. If you couldn't hold on to the promise of the rainbow, you deserved to be out in the rain. I felt my life sentence as a renegade was to wander incessantly in the darkness of my own despair. I couldn't have been more wrong. Not only was God with me in the darkness, but was holding my hand, guiding me back home.

I've learned in my time in the valley, peering across the horizon, often longing for home, what the late American novelist Frederick Buechner once observed, "Faith is homesickness. Faith is a lump in the throat; it is less a position on than a movement toward."[54] I once believed that I had to walk through the darkness alone and afraid, but now I know that I never once walked alone, and you haven't either. He was beside you all along, even when you couldn't tell.

REFLECTION QUESTIONS

1. With hindsight I've learned that struggling with doubt while grappling with loss is not apostasy; it is just human. This was certainly true of me upon hearing the news of my mother's brush with death. It is only human to doubt everything you thought you once knew when your whole world comes crashing down. Are you grappling with loss presently? Or possibly unprocessed grief from the past?

2. Imminent death has an uncanny ability to quickly cut through the veneer of our faith and expose the utter frailty of our beliefs. I wish someone had told me at the start of my own struggle with faith in college that it is human to doubt, and that doubt feels a lot like fear. Change is supposed to feel like something is off, because something is. Are you struggling with your faith, or just being human? There is a difference.

3. For those of us who grew up in the church, questioning the truth of Christianity can feel almost like a betrayal. Feeling like renegades, many of us choose to live as expats riddled with shame in a self-imposed exile. We find ourselves spiritual refugees displaced somewhere between faith and doubt, taking asylum by default in agnosticism, because somehow we come to believe faith is opposed to doubt and not actually part of the process. Do you feel that way? Does this chapter alleviate some of that pressure or shame you may be carrying?

4. Jesus said on one occasion that we must be born again spiritually to enter the kingdom of heaven, and on another, that we must become like little children. If the

conception of faith can be compared to birth and puberty, then salvation is always going to be something of a mess. I haven't met a teen who hasn't rebelled against their parents or challenged their authority. So why should we think spiritual adolescents will be any different? How does this framework change the way you identify where you are in your own faith journey today?

A PRAYER

A Hymn in the face of loss and grief:

"It is well with my Soul."[55]

When peace like a river, attendeth my way,
When sorrows like sea billows roll;
Whatever my lot, Thou hast taught me to know
It is well, it is well, with my soul.

It is well, (it is well),
With my soul, (with my soul)
It is well, it is well, with my soul.

Though Satan should buffet, though trials should come,
Let this blest assurance control,
That Christ has regarded my helpless estate,
And hath shed His own blood for my soul.

It is well, (it is well),
With my soul, (with my soul)
It is well, it is well, with my soul.

Chapter 4
Pride and Prejudice

*"Travel is fatal to prejudice, bigotry and narrow-
mindedness and many of our people need it
sorely on these accounts."*
Mark Twain

HOW POSTMODERNISM IS REMAKING THE WORLD

The *Handmaid's Tale* by Margaret Atwood—prolific
Canadian novelist, past Guggenheim fellow and twice
recipient of the Brooker prize—has seen an astonishing revival since its initial debut close to forty years ago. A
revived symbol of defiance and women's empowerment in the
advent of the #MeToo Movement, this 1985 classic has once
again topped the bestselling charts, also becoming an Emmy
Award-winning TV series produced by Hulu, the first streaming service ever to win an Emmy for best television series and
female lead (Elisabeth Moss).

The Handmaid's Tale is a novel about a near dystopian future where the human race is on the precipice of disaster. The near complete collapse of fertility rates due to rampant sexually transmitted disease, in tandem with environmental pollution, has left humanity close to extinction. As a result, a totalitarian theocracy called the Republic of Gilead—a Christian extremist group—overthrows the US government and becomes the sole inheritor of what was formerly known as the United States of America. This new regime moves rapidly to consolidate its power, overtaking all other faith groups, including all conventional Christian denominations. The new regime reorganizes society along the lines of a bizarre Old Testament interpretation, in which women are completely stripped of their human rights, including autonomy over their own reproductive function. A neo ultra-model of patriarchy is constructed that brutally subjugates most women to work as "handmaids" to bear children for the commanders who belong to the ruling class.

In light of the social and political turmoil in the world today, such speculation about a dystopian future rings all too true, and this is precisely why Atwood's classic is so frightening. This once distant cautionary tale no longer feels merely cautionary. In fact, it feels a little too close for comfort. According to a recent Pew Research study, trust in institutions is at historical lows in the United States. The study reveals only about one-quarter of Americans say they trust the government in Washington to do what is right "just about always" (2%) or "most of the time" (22%), in contrast to a time in the past when three-quarters of Americans trusted the federal government to do the right thing almost always (75%) or most of the time (75%). This is an almost complete reversal in just half a century of American public life. David Brooks writes about the law of unintended consequences when trust is eroded in the moral fabric of society in a piece for the *Atlantic*:

> Social trust is a measure of the moral quality of a society—of whether the people and institutions in it are trustworthy, whether they keep their promises and work for the common good. When people in a church lose faith or trust in God, the church collapses. When people in a society lose faith or trust in their institutions and in each other, the nation collapses.[56]

As a result, the broader culture today generally has a deeply embedded suspicion of religions, institutions, and power. It is particularly wary of exclusive truth claims that proffer an overarching narrative about absolutes. Most view these claims as nothing more than manipulation by those in power to stay in power. Perhaps more than any other, postmodernism may be the most resonant and dominant cultural narrative shaping culture today.

Especially relevant to our discussion is how this new powerful cultural narrative is remaking the world as Christianity wanes; and how an embedded mistrust of institutions is remaking the church in an age when truth is relegated to individual tribes. How does the church function in an age where its story has become one of many and no longer the central one, Where doubt is valued over compliance, autonomy over authority, and relativity over absolutes? In a sense, we all have exhaled modernity and inhaled post-modernity. Whether we are conscious of it or not, the world has changed, and it has changed forever. The old is gone and the new has come, and we now reside in a post-Christian world.

Perhaps it is not surprising that along with the recent passing of Billy Graham, the era of biblical authority in America has also passed. In Graham's era, not only did about 75 percent of the US population attend church, but the majority also believed the Bible to be the authoritative word of God.[57] Today, church attendance is precipitously in decline and along with church history, the Bible has become for many just a collection of archaic fables from a time long gone.

REVISIONIST HISTORY

My fondest memories as a doctoral student at the University of Pennsylvania are of the frequent field trips with colleagues on a chartered bus, where we'd chat away with a glass of rosé in one hand and cheese and crackers in the other. While I do believe laughter and fine wine make the heart grow fonder, sometimes on that bus we also debated hot button topics: politics and matters of faith and religion.

In one of those conversations one colleague said that he believed that Dan Brown makes a compelling case about Christianity in *The Da Vinci Code*—that it is an institution built on a historically fraudulent precedent with the primary aim of consolidating power. Most present considered this simply as a matter of opinion, and it went in one ear and out the other, but as someone who had actually studied the history of Christianity in seminary, I was stunned that anyone trained in one of the best research universities in the world could accept such interpretations as facts.

I had to restrain myself, because I knew there are a plethora of examples people can choose from both past and present that can easily discredit the witness of the church. The Crusades for one, that burning people alive thing, or even a couple of shady televangelists would suffice. Citing a work of fiction jammed with historical inaccuracies is not what I would have chosen as the best means of doing so, however. That would be the moral equivalent of citing *The Hitchhiker's Guide to the Galaxy* as a reason for doubting NASA, and arguing Douglas Adams makes a compelling case for the existence of alien life, not only in the known universe, but right here on earth.

The *New York Times* writer Laura Miller described Dan Brown's novel as "based on a notorious hoax," "rank nonsense," and "bogus," saying it is heavily based on the fabrications of Pierre Plantard, asserted to have created the Priory of Sion in 1956.[58] For the same reason, Margaret Atwood had a bone to pick with the media's classification of her book in a recent interview. She was adamant that, contrary to popular opinion, *The Handmaid's Tale* is not science fiction, but speculative fiction. So what is the difference? Well, simply that science fiction gives writers license to be almost completely untethered from reality, while speculative fiction does not.

For example, we know for certain that Predator and Alien are not in Cairo fighting for ultimate supremacy inside the pyramids, nor will they ever do so. This is why numerous critics took issue with the quality of Dan Brown's research in the novel. It is apparent that he was influenced more by his own embedded suspicions than by actual events of history, into which he did not bother to inquire. Instead, he used fiction disguised as historical fact to advance his conjectures.

PRIDE AND PREJUDICE

Nevertheless, with hindsight, I now realize that regardless of our position, whether that of a scholar or a middle schooler, all of us without exception have unfounded presuppositions that we believe are true regardless of the facts. It's called "implicit bias" for a reason. We all do this at a subatomic level almost subconsciously, and that is precisely my point: how much of what we know and believe about Christianity is made up of presuppositions which, unlike facts, have simply never been challenged?

A good example of this type of bias is Richard Dawkins' relentless attacks on Christian theology and Christian practices, without having any expertise in either, apart from his own prejudices. As mentioned earlier, he once infamously had printed in bold on the cover of his book the notion that God is a "delusion." In response to Dawkins, Alister McGrath, Andreos Idreos Professor of Science and Religion at the University of Oxford, who initially studied natural science at Oxford, earning a doctorate in molecular biophysics then an additional doctorate in historical theology, writes:

> Dawkins' analysis here is unacceptable. There are points at which his ignorance of religion ceases to be amusing, and simply becomes risible. Many Christian readers of this will be astonished at this bizarre misrepresentation of things being presented

as if it were gospel truth. It's about as worthwhile as trying to persuade a flat-earther that the world is actually round. Dawkins seems to be so deeply trapped within his own worldview that he cannot assess alternatives.[59]

In Dawkins' own words, faith, no matter how sincere or treasured, is a delusion. In *The God Delusion,* Dawkins mocks prayer, equating it with calling upon a sky fairy.[60] Did Dawkins arrive at these conclusions as a good scientist would, after a fastidious analysis of historical theology or even a sincere inquiry into the claims Christianity is making? Clearly not, because you can't take something seriously or sincerely if you have already decided it is a sham. Affirming a verdict apart from inquiry is not only poor form, but poor science. It also demonstrates one's own partiality to something other than the truth. In Dawkins' case, it is a horrid confluence of hubris and bias, as he postures to advance his own worldview.

Even Isaac Newton, who is widely recognized as perhaps the most influential scientist of all time and a key figure in the scientific revolution, and who would not be considered an orthodox Christian by today's standards, believed the laws that governed the universe were created by the divine. His book, *Philosophia Naturalis Principia Mathematica* ("Mathematical Principles of Natural Philosophy"), first published in 1687, laid the foundations of classical mechanics and was a precursor to modern science. Although most consider the laws of motion and universal gravitation as Newton's magnum opus, Newton himself cautioned against seeing the universe as a mere machine, akin to a great clock. He wrote: "So then gravity may put the planets into motion, but without the Divine Power, it could never put them into such a circulating motion, as they have about the sun."[61]

In addition, Francis Collins, director of the National Institute of Health tells a drastically different story about the time he was confronted with the possibility of belief as a third-year medical student in Chapel Hill, North Carolina. He recounts in *The Language of God* that his most awkward moment came when an older woman, suffering daily from severe untreatable angina, asked him what he believed:

> It was a fair question; we had discussed many other important issues of life and death, and she had shared her own strong Christian beliefs with me. I felt my face flush as I stammered out the words "I'm not really sure." Her obvious surprise brought into sharp relief a predicament that I had been running away from for nearly all of my twenty-six years: I had never really seriously considered the evidence for and against belief. That moment haunted me for several days. Did I not consider myself a scientist? Does a scientist draw conclusions without considering the data? Could there be a more important question in all of human existence than "Is there a God?" And yet there I found myself, with a combination of willful blindness and something that could only be properly described as arrogance, having avoided any serious consideration that God might be a real possibility. Suddenly all my arguments seemed very

thin, and I had the sensation that the ice under my
feet was cracking.[62]

Francis Collins' journey to faith was nevertheless a long
and winding road. He recounts that before entering med
school and while completing his doctorate in Biochemistry
at Yale, he "felt quite comfortable challenging the spiritual
beliefs of anyone who mentioned them in [his] presence and
discounted such perspectives as sentimentality and outmoded
superstition,"[63] until the faith of an elderly woman in Chapel
Hill suffering with an untreatable ailment somehow made his
atheism uncomfortable.

Nonetheless, for those of us who grew up outside the church,
this is the story we often find ourselves in. We may have no ill
will toward religion, but simply feel comfortable in our willful blindness and implicit bias towards matters of belief. At the
same time, this means that most of us have not rejected faith
outright, but have merely dismissed the idea that it might be
relevant to us. Rejection and dismissal are two different phe-
nomena. The former means that there was an actual investigation, but the latter suggests this question was simply overlooked.
Understanding the difference is important.

I've experienced this type of willful blindness and implicit
bias firsthand because this is exactly what happened to my wife
and I when we first met. My wife once told me I wasn't her
type. I agreed with her that she was definitely not into the "hot
type," but to her surprise, she eventually gave in and married
me. Jane's Austen's *Pride and Prejudice* is perhaps the greatest love story ever written, because Elizabeth and Mr. Darcy's

smugness lead to a contriteness that ultimately paves the way for some of the most intoxicating and romantic dialogue in the history of English literature. How else do we explain lines like, "You have bewitched my heart and soul," or "One word shall silence me forever."

Pride and prejudice are Victorian attitudes now repeated in a postmodern age. Sometimes, life's greatest joys and surprises come into our lives when we are wrong. Saul became Paul and went from jailing and murdering other Christians to becoming perhaps the greatest Christian witness the world has ever known, writing nearly half the New Testament himself. C. S. Lewis went from being a pugnacious atheist who ridiculed the idea of God in the halls of Oxford to the greatest Christian intellectual and apologist of the twentieth century. Addressing the skepticism many secular people have about Christianity, Tim Keller suggests it is only fair that the same double standard we often use to judge opposing views should be applied to us well:

> The only way to doubt Christianity rightly and fairly is to discern the alternate belief under each of your doubts and then to ask yourself what reasons you have for believing it. How do you know your belief is true? It would be inconsistent to require more justification for Christian belief than you do for your own, but that is frequently what happens. In fairness you must doubt your doubts. My thesis is that if you come to recognize the beliefs on which your doubts about Christianity are based, and if you seek as much proof for those beliefs as you seek from Christians

for theirs—you will discover that your doubts are not
as solid as they first appeared.[64]

In conversations with secular friends over recent years, I
have repeatedly encountered one particular stereotype: "I always
thought Christians were generally dumb." In my experience, the
primary reason those who live in global cities dismiss Christianity altogether is because of this single generalized assumption. I
have experienced this attitude firsthand, as secular friends who
visit our church are often astounded to meet so many thinking
Christians: physicians in multiple specialties; engineers who
work at Google and Amazon; lead actors in HBO Max animated
shorts programs for Warner Brothers; and students at Columbia
or NYU. Clearly Christians aren't unintelligent, but the power of
unchecked bias can overwhelm common sense.

Eliminating this stereotype requires something powerful.
Sometimes representation of Christianity is limited to what we
see depicted on the news. Yet, with over two billion adherents,
fringe movements within Christianity do exist, and the media
usually only focuses on these. Most families have an odd uncle
or family member that maybe drinks a little too much and blurts
out obscenities at odd times, and the church is no exception. We
love our uncle, we really do, but we're also horrified every time
he opens his mouth.

I thus attempt in this book to highlight the most underrep-
resented group within ecumenical Christianity: Christians in
elite secular institutions in large secular cities today studying
or conducting groundbreaking research; Christian physicians in
multiple specialties flourishing in their work in the city, recon-

structing public opinion about the value of faith in one's personal life and in healthcare; Christian engineers working at top tech companies seeking to solve the world's greatest problems. Mark Twain once said that "travel is fatal to prejudice, bigotry and narrow-mindedness and many of our people need it sorely on these accounts. Broad, wholesome, charitable views of men and things cannot be acquired by vegetating in one little corner of the earth all one's lifetime."[65]

The world's biggest problems currently stem largely from miscommunication. From two boys fighting behind a schoolyard and two nations on the brink of war, the festering wound that endangers the survival of our species is not explicit violence, but implicit bias. The real danger is not what we say in the public square, but the views we harbor in isolation. If we cannot genuinely listen to opposing views and assume we're right apart from sincere dialogue, we're not perpetuating real tolerance, just greater ignorance, which ultimately leads to greater prejudice, leaving our world far poorer and more precarious.

SURPRISED BY JOY

Bagel (his choice of pseudonym) was also surprised by Christianity and even more stunned when he became one. After getting baptized he joined a community he would have considered brainwashed just a few years earlier. Bagel's faith story began with the many assumptions he had about Christianity. He believed Christians were like the Walking Dead—brainwashed zombies indoctrinated into believing in anti-science religious dogma, such as creationism. With his natural leanings towards science, he believed this ridiculous. How could the entire universe have been made in seven days when official data from the Planck space observatory proves it is at least 13.8 billion years old! Sure, there might be some disparities, but that was too much of a gap, and so he dismissed Christianity outright. How could anyone be off by almost 14 billion years?

On the day of his baptism ceremony, Bagel shared some of the views he had held about Christians: Growing up in the suburbs of Chicago, he always assumed that church was primarily a social club where his Korean school friends went on weekends, much like the popular Canadian sitcom "Kim's Convenience," about a Korean immigrant family living in a Toronto suburb. He also thought Christians were generally weird and most likely social outcasts. Why else would you give up your entire weekend unless you have no friends? Again, it came as a surprise to Bagel when in college, he met a girl at a party he thought was pretty cute. She turned out to be a Christian and invited him to church. Yes, what is humorous about his story is that only a cute girl could skirt his biases and defenses.

Bagel's faith journey continued when he moved to downtown Manhattan to attend the prominent NYU Tisch School of Performing Arts, where he studied film and television. He began battling severe bouts of depression, loneliness, and rage. He often questioned the purpose of continuing his humdrum and dreadful existence and confessed during his baptism ceremony that he had vowed that if he wasn't happy by thirty, he would bid farewell to this world and end it all. He shared that he always believed that the church only had space in its rows for those who believed, but it turned out he was wrong again. He learned that the invitation of the gospel is a promise of safe harbor for all those who doubt and weep and those who are barely holding on and ripping at the seams. Jesus invites all those who are weary to come to him and fall apart and find rest. In tears, Bagel said "that is when I knew I belonged, and when I knew I was finally home."

If we truly want to learn and discover anything new, we must check our assumptions at the door, or they will sabotage our voyage even before it begins. The truth is that faith, along with anything else, is not what it appears from a distance. You only get to truly grasp something up close. True civility is tested not in the absence of disagreements, but despite them. If diversity is truly treasured, we can have unity apart from uniformity. This is always the real test of civility, and even if we ultimately disagree in the end, at least we'll both be better for having walked in someone else's shoes.

REFLECTION QUESTIONS

1. Postmodernism is perhaps the most dominant narrative shaping culture today. As a result, the broader culture generally has a deeply embedded suspicion of religions, institutions, and power. It is particularly wary of exclusive truth claims. Most view these claims as nothing more than manipulation by those in power to stay in power. Do you have an inherent mistrust or embedded suspicion of religious institutions and their leaders? Why or why not? Please explain.

2. Francis Collins' journey to faith was long and winding. He recounts that before entering med school and while completing his doctorate in Biochemistry at Yale, he "felt quite comfortable challenging the spiritual beliefs of anyone who mentioned them in [his] presence and discounted such perspectives as sentimentality and outmoded superstition," until the faith of an elderly woman in Chapel Hill suffering an untreatable ailment somehow made his atheism uncomfortable. Where are you in your journey?

3. For those who grew up outside the church, many have not rejected faith outright, but have merely dismissed the idea that it might be relevant. Rejection and dismissal are two different things. The former means that there was an actual investigation, but the latter suggests this question was simply overlooked. Understanding the difference is important. Do you recognize this willful blindness in your own life?

4. Bagel's faith story began with the many assumptions he had about Christianity. He believed Christians were

brainwashed zombies, indoctrinated into believing in anti-science religious dogma, such as creationism. How much of what you know and believe about Christianity is made up of biases like this, getting in the way of truly having an open heart and mind?

A PRAYER

Jane Austen pointing to our often-explicit blindness to our pride and prejudice:

"Your defect is a propensity to hate everybody." "And yours," he replied with a smile, "is willfully to misunderstand them."[66]

Jane Austen, Pride and Prejudice

PART III:
FAITH IN PRACTICE

Chapter 5

The Origin Question: Did God Really Create the World?

"Gravity may put the planets into motion, but without the Divine Power, it could never put them into such a circulating motion, as they have about the sun."
Isaac Newton

I once read a headline in the *New York Times* that really caught my attention: "Elon Musk's Plan: Get Humans to Mars, and Beyond."[67] The headline seems more appropriate for the entertainment section than for a feature in the daily science segment. The article covered the 67th International Astronautical Congress in Guadalajara, Mexico, in 2016, where SpaceX unveiled plans for interplanetary space travel over the upcoming quarter century. Musk claimed that the first passengers to Mars could take off as soon as 2024, if everything went without a hitch. It won't be long before a mars candy bar becomes the snack of choice and "The Martian" is every passenger's favorite in-flight movie.

When science fiction transcends fantasy and begins to flirt with reality, it can really awaken one's imagination. C. S. Lewis noted that "reason is the natural organ of truth, but imagination is the organ of meaning. Imagination, producing new metaphors or revivifying old, is not the cause of truth, but its condition."[68] The truth is that our culture's desperate search for meaning points to a haunting in all of us that is almost primordial. It is simply instinctive for us to seek meaning outside of ourselves, since we know for certain that we are living in a story we did not write. G. K. Chesterton once put it this way: "I had always felt life first as a story: and if there is a story, there is a story-teller."[69]

But who is responsible for this story we all find ourselves in? Who or what is responsible for the vast diversity of life on earth from which all life originates? In short, the origin question is the ultimate question humanity has been grappling with ever since achieving sentience through the evolution of consciousness. Did God really create the world, or was it all simply a derivative of binary probability? Is the world merely a generated sequence of zeros and ones, or is it perhaps a simulation embedded in a metaverse by an advanced alien civilization, as some have recently mused? Understanding the origin of the universe is of paramount importance in unraveling the full story behind our own genesis.

This angst and search for meaning is the "Holy Haunting" I explored in Chapter Two. If we use this beautiful theological reality as our primary lens, we'll recognize that our culture is actually giving us the key to its heart. It is the very key we need to unlock the buried treasure within the human soul. In the past, we were (and sometimes still are) haunted by the transcendence of sex. As mid-twentieth century Scottish writer Bruce Marshall once suggested, "Every man knocking on a brothel is looking for God."[70] Similarly, everyone looking for aliens or UFOs is looking for God. The object has changed, but not the desire. We must recognize our culture's obsession with the paranormal as a holy haunting, rather than the rise of whacked-out conspiracy theories. We can only begin to understand the hearts of others when we begin to value and respect their journeys.

This is precisely the reason our culture is so captivated by the metaphysical. We are obsessed with any other world external to our own. It is an obsession that goes from the Marvel Universe to documentaries on ancient aliens building pyramids, and continues on to a fascination with the discovery via NASA's Hubble Telescope of a gargantuan ocean called Europa on one of Jupiter's moons. This will be the next frontier in interplanetary space travel, after touching down on Mars, according to Musk's interview in Mexico. Imagination is scratching an itch that reason cannot satisfy; in a subtle manner, Star Wars, the X-Files, and Battlestar Galactica do not seem to be entirely far-fetched.

In conversations across many years, secular friends and seekers have often mused about the origin of life, sharing their difficulties in taking Christianity seriously at first, mainly because it seems so anti-science. They found it difficult to reconcile their view of faith as mythological and science as empirical. Science and faith were seen as competing, even adversarial worldviews. The greatest hurdle was "Creationism," or the manner in which the biblical creation narrative has often been understood. One particular seeker asked how the entire universe could have been made in seven days, when official data from the Planck Space Observatory proves it is at least 13.8 billion years old. Another joked that an advanced ancient civilization was more likely to have created the big bang than a supreme deity.

Interest in the paranormal increases as NASA continues to discover additional exoplanets. In response, new and more creative conspiracy theories dominate the headlines and continue to capture the hearts of an entire generation. Perhaps theories about ancient aliens and UFOs excite the imagination of our culture, because the church's communication of the metaphysical is too sterile. Although the Book of Genesis clearly tells us that God created the earth after the heavens, we skim over cosmology and move on to anthropology too quickly in our theology. Yet, if our creation narrative cannot surpass those of SpaceX, Marvel and Star Wars, those stories will appear to be more reasonable alternatives than the God of Abraham. For this reason, in this chapter, I revisit the creation narrative found in the Book of Genesis, with the goal of painting a holistic picture of life's origins that is both biblically accurate and scientifically satisfying.

WHAT THE BIBLE TELLS US ABOUT CREATION

Genesis 1:1 asserts, "In the beginning, God created the heavens and the earth." There are three things the very first verse of the Bible tells us about the nature of God, the universe, and the earth respectively. First, it introduces the preeminence of God, the one who has no origin and exists independently of the time-space continuum. The first verse posits quite literally that in the beginning there was God. Second, the origin of the universe is clearly attributed to God's celestial artistry: "God created the heavens." Lastly, earth was created after God created the universe: "God created the heavens and the earth." Hence, a faithful reading of the Book of Genesis begins with cosmology, because creation begins with the cosmos, and not the earth.

Many scholars agree that Moses and his later editors were responsible for inspiring the contents of the first five books of the Bible, known as the Pentateuch. The biblical author of the creation account deliberately chose to utilize poetic imagery to portray the origin of the universe and the earth. This would have made sense, especially to a primarily Jewish audience, since the tradition of the Pentateuch, also known as the Torah, was passed down through a sacred rite of oral tradition in an unbroken chain from one generation to another. Even today, some orthodox Jews are able to recite the entire Pentateuch verbatim from memory, since it is considered the most sacred text in Judaism.

This historical framework is vital to understanding Moses' intention of creating an oral history of the creation account of the God of Abraham, Isaac and Jacob that we now have in its present literary form. Even a sacred text such as the Book of Genesis is not written in a vacuum, but is rather embedded in a cultural context. Thus, a faithful reading of the Book of Genesis requires an understanding that the biblical account of creation is as much a literary work as it is divinely inspired.

As previously noted, one of the greatest barriers preventing so many of those living in a post-Christian world from taking Christianity seriously is the creation narrative infamously known as Creationism. Creationists hold to a seven-day origin of the universe and the earth based on a very literal interpretation of the creation account found in Genesis. Earth creationists believe that a faithful reading of the Bible should lead Christians to accept that the earth is young, just somewhere between 6,000 and 10,000 years old. In addition, as the Biologos foundation points out, "Creationism claims that Scripture is not compatible with the concept that humans share common ancestry with other life forms on earth, and most creationists believe that evolution is a direct threat to Christianity."[71]

Nevertheless, in light of both scientific and biblical evidence, Creationism leads to poor science, and even poorer theology, because it builds an entire worldview on origins out of issues the Bible never directly addresses. A faithful reading of Scripture only tells us that God created the world, but it doesn't tell us how. When it comes to answering life's ultimate questions, such as why we're here in the first place, or why we seek to make meaning at all, science becomes silent. Science answers questions of "how," while theology addresses the "why." This is not because science is opposed to faith, but rather because science has no parameters for such an inquiry; and it is critical to acknowledge the difference.

The Bible in its entirety does not make scientific statements. It makes ontological statements that cannot be empirically proven or disproven. Thus, any hypothetical timeline of the origin of the universe is always an inference based on factors outside of the Bible. The way that Creationists reach a "young earth" interpretation breaks the most basic rule in biblical exegesis, i.e., never insert your own presuppositions and bias into a reading of the text. Seek instead to understand the author's initial intent through a critical study and objective analysis.

EVOLUTIONARY CREATIONISM

Clearly, Moses did not witness the formation of the primordial universe firsthand, because he wasn't there in the first place. Thus, the account of the origin of the universe found in Genesis cannot be a literal account, but is instead a literary representation of the creation through the power of story and imagery. What we do know for certain is that the creation account in the Pentateuch is thought to date back to 600 BC, "when existing oral and written traditions were brought together to form books recognizable as those we now know, reaching their final form around 400 BC."[72]

Consequently, a faithful reading of Scripture requires comprehending that the sacred text is just as much a literary work as it is divinely inspired. This leads back to a rigorous and critical pursuit of a better understanding of the creation narrative as found in the Book of Genesis in its present literary form. Subsequently, when we begin to read the Book of Genesis through a literary lens, we begin to recognize that Moses and his later editors deliberately chose to integrate literary devices in their portrayal of the creation event. For example, the word "day" in Hebrew is *yom* (Hebrew: יֹם), which refers to an undefined period of time, or, as explained by Archer L. Gleason, former Professor of Old Testament and Semitics at Trinity Evangelical Divinity School, directly translates to an "extended period" or "age." He writes:

> Hebrew expresses "the first day" by *hayyom harison*, but this text says simply *yom ehad* (day one). Again, in v.8 we read not *hayyom hasseni* ("the second day")

but *yom seni* ("a second day"). In Hebrew prose of this genre, the definite article was generally used where the noun was intended to be definite; only in poetic style could it be omitted. The same is true with the rest of the six days; they all lack the definite article. Thus they are well adapted to a sequential pattern, rather than to strictly delimited units of time.[73]

This is the reason a literal interpretation doesn't always yield the correct interpretation, because sometimes words are defined more by their surrounding context than by a straightforward meaning. Thus, a faithful reading of Genesis does not warrant or equate to a literal seven-day creation phenomenon as some creationists and literalists assume. In fact, Francis Collins, the former director of the National Institute of Health and founder of Biologos, introduces an alternative Christian position on origins he refers to as "evolutionary creationism." According to Collins:

> Evolutionary creation takes the Bible seriously as the inspired and authoritative word of God, and it takes science seriously as a way of understanding the world God has made. Evolutionary creation includes two basic ideas. First, that God created all things, including human beings in his own image. Second, that evolution is the best scientific explanation we currently have for the diversity and similarities of all life on Earth.[74]

Evolutionary creationism portrays a vivid picture of life's origins that is both biblically true and scientifically satisfying. It creates a beautiful image of the innumerous complexities that are weaved into the very fabric of the universe, in tandem with all the diversity of life, both seen and unseen. In the words of T. S. Eliot, "at the end of all our exploring we will arrive at the place we started and know the place for the first time."[75] Such a view compels and stokes the imagination of both the seeker and believer. It is a perspective of the cosmos that is so elegant and exquisite that it leaves one in complete awe. It is worship for the believer and wonder for the seeker. Robert Jastrow, an agnostic astrophysicist, writes:

> At this moment it seems as though science will never be able to raise the curtain on the mystery of creation. For the scientist who has lived by his faith in the power of reason, the story ends like a bad dream. He has scaled the mountains of ignorance; he is about to conquer the highest peak; as he pulls himself over the final rock, he is greeted by a band of theologians who have been sitting there for centuries.[76]

Francis Su, Benediktsson-Karwa Professor of Mathematics at Harvey Mudd College, former president of the Mathematical Association of America, author of Mathematics for Human Flourishing, and winner of the 2021 Euler Book Prize, was recently invited by Big Think and the John Templeton Foundation to write a piece on the similarities between math and religion, and in so doing he noticed a rather surprising commonality. He writes:

> In both mathematical and spiritual pursuits, one perceives truths of such transcendent depth that they

evoke awe and veneration. The dignity of human beings, the corrupting nature of sin, the importance of justice, and the power of forgiveness are all truths that can be felt profoundly in a religious experience. Similarly, encounters with the beauty of symmetry or a deep connection between disparate ideas in mathematics can elicit profound astonishment in mathematical experiences. Sometimes these encounters are only glimpses, hints that something exists that is both greater and unseen.[77]

Indiana, a Stanford trained engineer at Google whom I recently had the awesome privilege of baptizing at my church at 180, experienced a similar pattern in his own faith journey. He said that one major catalyst that led him to belief was the incalculable complexity that is woven into the very fabric of the universe, in tandem with all the diversity of life, both seen and unseen. In short, a perspective of the cosmos that is so elegant and opulent that it led him to worship. These are Indiana's own words on the day of his baptism:

From a scientific perspective, I could not accept that life was produced by random chance. Life is too complex, too difficult, too fragile. Scientists have discovered thousands of planets; none of them have the conditions to sustain even the simplest of living organisms. The fact that all of this was orchestrated seemed much more believable. I refused to believe that life was meaningless. What, we're here to just exist? What's the point in that? If that was all there was to life, humanity might as well just focus on reproducing, multiply like flies—or what was even the point in that? If humanity were gone, Earth would still be here. And flies, well, you better believe they'd still be here, we can't get them out of our homes as it is. We must be here for a reason.

Therefore, ironically, when a skeptic asks with their usual defiance, and with the aim of highlighting the absurdity of the position, how the Bible can possibly argue that God created the entire universe in seven days when the scientific data shows it is 14 billion years old, my short answer is, "it doesn't, and it never did, but many assume it does." First, the question is a false equivalency, because it offers one truth and one lie. Although the scientific data is correct, the biblical assumption is not, for the Bible only claims that God created the universe, not how God did so.

In addition, understanding the account of the origin of the universe in its literary form in the Book of Genesis leaves ample room for science to explain how the universe began in an ultra-hot dense state, ballooned and stretched out. Astrophysicist Andrew May describes the Big Bang this way:

[F]irst at unimaginable speeds, and then at a more measurable rate—over the next 13.8 billion years to the still-expanding cosmos that we know today. When cosmic inflation came to a sudden and still-mysterious end, the more classic descriptions of the Big Bang took hold. A flood of matter and radiation, known as "reheating," began populating our universe with the stuff we know today: particles, atoms, the stuff that would become stars and galaxies and so on.[78]

Accordingly, scientific theories such as the Big Bang that illuminate in vast detail the critical unfolding of the primordial universe help fill the gaps in our understanding where the Bible is silent. The biblical account of creation is not at all at odds with a model of cosmology within an expanding universe which we know today as the Big Bang theory. They are, in fact, remarkably complementary. Many have assumed that faith and science are at odds, that they are competing worldviews, and one must choose either/or when clearly Scripture allows for both/and. Yet again, and as mentioned in Chapter Two, the scope and framework of our inquiry doesn't have to be limited to our fancied binaries. Compared to the vastness of the universe, our epistemological differences are inconsequential, and our only allegiance should be to push the boundaries of human knowledge further than before.

In fact, the very construct and discovery of a model of an expanding universe—which is usually credited to Edwin Hubble, whose astronomical data was obtained from the velocity-distance relationship between galaxies—originated with a Belgian Catholic priest and MIT astronomer by the name of Georges Lemaître. Before Hubble-Lemaître's law was discovered, most scientists, including Einstein, believed in a static universe and assumed that the estimated 100 billion stars within the Milky Way composed the totality of the universe.

Ironically, although Hubble is credited with the concept of an expanding universe—coined Hubble's Law—he, along with Einstein and other giants in theoretical physics, did not in fact believe in an expanding model of cosmology. So, why all the confusion? It turns out that nearly two years before Hubble published his astronomical data of galaxies moving away from Earth at speeds proportional to their distance, Georges Lemaître published a seminal article on the expanding universe along with astronomical data in a relatively unknown scientific journal published in French in Belgium. It went unread and unnoticed, because French wasn't the dominant language in astronomy in the day.

However, on October 29, 2018, the International Astronomical Union voted in support of renaming Hubble's Law to "Hubble-Lemaître Law. According to Jonathan Lunine, director of the Cornell Center for Astrophysics and Planetary Science, and vice president of the Society of Catholic Scientists, "such a vote would take place today—during a time when science and faith are portrayed in the media as implacable foes—speaks to the remarkable character of Lemaître himself, the Belgian monsignor and astronomer who made a number of fundamental contributions to the science of cosmic structure and origins."[79]

The question most people ask after discovering Lemaître was the actual father of the Big Bang Theory, and in many ways modern cosmology, is, why did it take almost a hundred years for the world to recognize his contribution? According to Lunine, while the public was mesmerized with the notion of Lemaître's model of an expanding universe, and even more, that it was conceived by a Catholic priest, many of Lemaître's contemporaries were less thrilled. Exploring the life, faith and expanding universe theory of Georges Lemaître in a piece for the McGrath Institute for Church Life at the University of Notre Dame, Lunine writes:

> The universe having a beginning was scientifically unattractive, since it meant that some state of reality might not be accessible to scientific investigation. And it smacked of religion—a kind of scientific version of Genesis. Lemaître's religious identity is relevant here—at every talk I give on this subject audience members express surprise, even amazement, that a Catholic priest could be a scientist, let alone such a prominent one. Appropriately recognizing Lemaître's name in the history of astronomy, by accepting the recommendation of the IAU to use the term "Hubble-Lemaître law," will benefit scientist-believers and scientist-atheists alike. For the former, it strengthens our case that science and faith are compatible. And for the latter, it might just help remove the suspicion that Lemaître has been treated differently from his peers, both in his lifetime and thereafter, because of the collar he wore.[80]

When addressing the ongoing polarity between faith and science, Francis Collins asks a question of the modern era. In the age of cosmology, evolution, and the human genome, is there still the possibility of a richly satisfying harmony between scientific and spiritual worldviews? He writes:

I answer with a resounding yes! In my view, there is no conflict in being a rigorous scientist and a person who believes in a God who takes a personal interest in each one of us. Science's domain is to explore nature. God's domain is in the spiritual world, a realm not possible to explore with the tools and language of science. It must be examined with the heart, the mind, and the soul—and the mind must find a way to embrace both realms.[81]

Even Charles Darwin concedes in the *Origin of Species* that "there is grandeur in this view of life, with its several powers, having been originally breathed by the Creator into a few forms or into one; and that, whilst this planet has gone cycling on according to the fixed law of gravity, from so simple a beginning, endless forms most beautiful and most wonderful have been, and are being evolved."[82]

Although faith and science diverge in their details, both essentially reveal who we are in the deepest sense ontologically: beings forged in the corridors of eternity and predating the advent of the Big Bang and the primordial universe. Both seek to draw back the curtain of eternity. Thus, the rise of spiritual consciousness is not a byproduct of cultural forces as many assume, but is rather an echo reverberating from eternity. Faith is the echo and eternity is the origin. Addressing the wondrous connectiveness of all creation, Collins writes, "nearly all of the atoms in your body were once cooked in the nuclear furnace of an ancient supernova—you are truly made of stardust."[83]

I mentioned at the start that understanding the origin of the universe is vital to unraveling the story behind our own. The origin question is the ultimate question humanity has been grappling with since achieving sentience in the evolution of human consciousness. In fact, a part of the theological mystery of humanity being endowed with such astonishing cognitive faculties is a signpost to being made in the image of God. The Biologos Foundation writes, "one view is that the image of God refers to uniquely human cognitive abilities. When people talk of the things that 'make us human,' they often refer to abilities like reason and rationality, mathematics and language, laughter and emotions, care and empathy, and cultural products such as music and art."[84]

In short, our sentience is a hereditary consequence of evolutionary creation and of being made in the image of the Creator, and not a derivative of binary probability generated by a sequence of zeros and ones. I wonder if the dream of becoming an interplanetary species and our desperate search for life in the oceans of Europa on one of Jupiter's moons or in the Martian desert is because we know this to be true in the deepest part of us: we are not alone in the universe, and that is what ultimately fuels our search. A holy haunting.

REFLECTION QUESTIONS

1. G. K. Chesterton once said: "I had always felt life first as a story: and if there is a story, there is a story-teller." But who is responsible for this story we all find ourselves in? Who or what is responsible for the vast diversity of life on earth from which all life originates? Where are you in this conversation?

2. In conversations over many years, secular friends and seekers have often mused about the origin of life, all sharing their difficulties taking Christianity seriously at first, mainly because it seemed so anti-science. For this reason, I tried to paint a holistic picture of life's origins that is both biblically accurate and scientifically satisfying. Do you believe that goal was achieved in this chapter, or that it at least shifted your thinking to the possibility of faith and science being companions rather than implacable foes?

3. For many seekers, the greatest hurdle taking Christianity seriously is "Creationism," or the way the biblical creation narrative has often been understood. Did it surprise you to learn that Genesis never posits a literal seven-day creation account in the original Hebrew? Or that a Belgian Catholic Priest called Georges Lemaître is the father of modern cosmology and the big bang theory?

4. Charles Darwin concedes in the *Origin of Species* that "there is grandeur in this view of life, with its several powers, having been originally breathed by the Creator into a few forms or into one; and that, whilst this planet has gone cycling on according to the fixed law of

gravity, from so simple a beginning, endless forms most beautiful and most wonderful have been, and are being evolved." Did that surprise you at all, coming as it does from Darwin?

A PRAYER

The Glory of God revealed in Creation:

"There is grandeur in this view of life, with its several powers, having been originally breathed by the Creator into a few forms or into one; and that, whilst this planet has gone cycling on according to the fixed law of gravity, from so simple a beginning, endless forms most beautiful and most wonderful have been, and are being evolved." [85]

Charles Darwin, The Origin of Species

Chapter 6

The Historicity Question: Did Jesus of Nazareth Actually Exist?

"Regardless of what anyone may personally think or believe about him, Jesus of Nazareth has been the dominant figure in the history of Western Culture for almost 20 centuries. If it were possible, with some sort of super magnet, to pull up out of history every scrap of metal bearing at least a trace of his name, how much would be left?"

Jaroslav Pelikan

I n the summer of '99, a few years after the dissolution of the Soviet Union, I visited the Republic of Kazakhstan on a mission trip. We stayed in the homes of local Kazakhstani believers who showed us tremendous hospitality during our stay, even though they did not have much to spare. Yet, notwithstanding, and being the spoiled American teenager, I was—accustomed to the modern conveniences and amenities of the first world—I had a very difficult time adjusting to life in the developing world.

It was a scorching hot summer and cold drinking water wasn't available, although ironically, cold showers were in ready supply. I learned a little too late that while Kazakhstan may be the ninth largest country in the world in terms of land-mass. It also has one of the lowest population densities (fewer than 15 people per square mile), and hence its irrigation and convenience stores are spotty and irregular. My Diet Coke with-drawal was horrid, and my mood was even worse! People must have thought I was very grumpy. I was too grumpy to care what they thought.

There are two critical things I've learned in hindsight about that summer. One is that I should probably never be a mission-ary. There was a real low point during my time there when I'd have probably sold my soul for some iced water. The other is the realization that I have a serious Diet Coke addiction, but no immediate plan to stop drinking it. After landing safely back at home, the first thing I did as a proud American teenager was eat a fat juicy burger, washed down with an icy cold Diet Coke, leaving thoughts of Kazakhstan behind, hopefully forever.

Yet, to my surprise, seven years later, Kazakhstan entered my life once again, and also the collective consciousness of the American public, when *Borat: Cultural Learnings of America for Make Benefit Glorious Nation of Kazakhstan,* a 2006 moc-kumentary, starring and co-written by Sacha Baron Cohen, was released to both acclaim and controversy. I couldn't believe my eyes watching Cambridge-educated Cohen playing the leading role of Borat Sagdiyev, a fictional Kazakhstani journalist—often featured on Da Ali G show on HBO prior—who travels from Kazakhstan and throughout the United States to make a documentary featuring real-life interactions with American public life. Much of the mockumentary features unscripted vignettes of Borat interviewing and mingling with bystanders who assume he is a foreigner with little or no understanding of American culture.

Although Cohen won numerous awards and acclaim for the satirical film, it was banned in Kazakhstan. Kazakh viewers and authorities did not like the way the film portrayed their country and culture, finding the stereotypes offensive, not to mention the behavior of the title character. In contrast to Cohen's portrayal, and according to the World Banks, Kazakhstan, has experienced a remarkable economic revival since my visit over twenty years ago: "Fueled by rapid growth and structural reforms, abundant hydrocarbon resources, strong domestic demand, and foreign direct investment (FDI), helped reduce poverty and transform the country into an upper-middle-income economy."[86]

However, speaking from personal experience, Cohen's mockumentary did more than just paint the Kazakhstani people in a satirical light. I actually met a freshman in college at my church who was fully convinced that the Republic of Kazakhstan didn't exist at all. He simply assumed that since Borat was clearly a fictional character and his country must be too! At first, I thought he was joking, but then I nearly choked on my burrito when I realized he was serious. The conversation went something like this:

Me: You know that Kazakhstan is a real country, right?
College Student: Ha! Very funny. No, it isn't.
Me: Dude, I went on a mission trip to Kazakhstan!

College Student: Stop playing. No, you didn't. It doesn't exist!

Me: Yes, I did, in the summer of 1999.

College student: Wait, really? Seriously?

Me: Yes! Did you really go to Staten Island Tech? (The 33rd ranked High School in the US, as reported by US News and World Report.)

College Student: Yes, but I really had no idea... I really thought the whole thing was satirical.

Me: Oh my God, isn't like Russian a perquisite at Tech?

College Student: (Gulp.) Yes, but we're really a STEM School.

Me: I guess they really don't teach geography in America anymore.

Later, I wondered how a college student who recently graduated from one of the top High Schools in the country—where Russian is taught as a foreign language—could assume that the ninth largest country in the world, and a former part of the Soviet Union just a few years prior, didn't exist, simply because of its association with a satirical film. But then again, as suggested previously, all of us, without exception, have beliefs that are made up of presuppositions which, unlike facts, have simply never been challenged. The more I thought about it, the more it made sense: how it was possible that the TikTok generation in the advent of social media could doubt the historicity of actual countries or other historical figures when mockumentaries such as *Borat* continue to blur the lines between fact and fiction. We are all susceptible to throwing the baby out with the bathwater and revising history.

THE QUEST FOR THE HISTORICAL JESUS

Similarly, some also argue that Jesus of Nazareth was doubly non-existent, suggesting that his existence is a mere hypothesis, that he is a Christian invention rather than a real historical figure. Did Jesus of Nazareth actually exist? Can his existence be confirmed and triangulated apart from the biased biblical sources? Are there any contemporary historians to corroborate his existence in the historical documents of early antiquity? These questions are not raised in academic circles, of course, for no serious historian questions the historicity of Jesus anymore. However, in the postmodern world of today, and since the advent of social media, these questions are whispered on the grapevines of a generation of laity who also question the existence of Helen Keller and the facticity of the lunar landing. Thus, this chapter explores the historicity of Jesus Nazareth through an ethnographical lens, reconstructing his life primarily through critical historical methods, in contrast to a personal religious interpretation.

Simon Gathercole, Professor of New Testament and Early Christianity at Cambridge University, discusses the evidence that Jesus Christ lived and died in a piece for the *Guardian* in which he makes the point that, oddly enough, the two leading historians arguing for the historicity of Jesus of Nazareth are non-Christians: "It is worth noting that the two mainstream historians who have written most against these hyper-skeptical arguments—against the historicity of Jesus as a historical figure—are atheists: Maurice Casey (formerly Nottingham University) and Bart Ehrman (University of North Carolina). They have issued stinging criticisms of the 'Jesus-myth' approach, branding it pseudo-scholarship."[87]

In addition, Elizabeth Livingstone, an Oxford theologian specializing in Patristics (the study of the early Christian writers who are designated as the Church Fathers) and F. L. Cross, the former Lady Margaret Professor of Divinity at the University of Oxford, note that the term "historical Jesus" refers to the reconstruction of the life and teachings of Jesus through a critical historical method of inquiry, in contrast to an interpretative approach.[88] Thus, one of the primary goals of historical criticism is to reconstruct the historical context in which the author of a text and its original recipients are embedded, by building a true description of the events that the text describes. Bart Ehrman notes the remarkable concord between Christian and secular historians on the understanding of Jesus of Nazareth as a real historical figure, as follows:

> Serious historians of the early Christian movement—
> all of them—have spent many years preparing to be
> experts in their field. Just to read the ancient sources
> requires expertise in a range of ancient languages:
> Greek, Hebrew, Latin, and often Aramaic, Syriac,
> and Coptic, not to mention the modern languages of
> scholarship (for example, German and French). And
> that is just for starters. Expertise requires years of
> patiently examining   ancient texts and a thor-
> ough grounding in the history and culture of Greek
> and Roman antiquity, the religions of the ancient
> Mediterranean world, both pagan and Jewish,
> knowledge of the history of the Christian church and
> the development of its social life and theology, and,

well, lots of other things. It is striking that virtually everyone who has spent all the years needed to attain these qualifications is convinced that Jesus of Nazareth was a real historical figure.[89]

Furthermore, Graham Stanton, Lady Margaret Professor of Divinity at the University of Cambridge, in addressing the non-historicity argument, concludes that, "today nearly all historians, whether Christians or not, accept that Jesus existed and that the gospels contain plenty of valuable evidence which has to be weighed and assessed critically. There is growing consensus that, with the possible exception of Paul, we know far more about Jesus of Nazareth than about any first or second century Jewish or pagan religious teacher."[90]

NON-CHRISTIAN SOURCES

Nearly all biblical scholars and classical historians of ancient antiquity and the Mediterranean world repudiate the theories claiming Jesus' non-existence, and perceive the hypothesis as a fringe theory with virtually no support among creditable scholars. Robert E. Van Voorst concludes, "The nonhistoricity thesis has always been controversial, and it has consistently failed to convince scholars of many disciplines and religious creeds. Biblical scholars and classical historians now regard it as effectively refuted."[91] Yet, perhaps the final straw to break the camel's back for the most ardent skeptic would be if Jesus' existence could be substantiated and triangulated apart from the bias of biblical sources.

Data triangulation is a research methodology applied in qualitative research to determine the location of a fixed point based on the laws of trigonometry. Such a law states that if one side and two angles of a triangle are known, the other two sides and angle of that triangle can be calculated. Dr. Deborah Rugg, Chief of the United Nations AIDS Monitoring and Evaluation Division, explains that data triangulation is the utilization of an array of data sources comprising time, space and persons. "Findings can be corroborated, and any weaknesses in the data can be compensated for by the strengths of other data, thereby increasing the validity and reliability of the results obtained. This approach has been applied in many sectors to strengthen conclusions about findings, and to reduce the risk of false interpretation."

Thus, to triangulate and determine the location of a fixed point in history that can support the truth about the existence of Jesus, I compare two non-biblical historical sources from two independent time periods with the canonical gospels in the New Testament. Since we have already established that nearly all biblical scholars and classical historians of ancient antiquity in the twenty-first first century corroborate Jesus' existence, the burden of proof remains with historians and other eye witnesses in ancient antiquity in the first and second century, and whether or not their accounts concur.

First, according to Peter Schäfer, Ronald O. Perelman Professor of Judaic Studies at Princeton University, "The Talmudic stories make fun of Jesus' birth from a virgin, fervently contest his claim to be the Messiah and Son of God and maintain that he was rightfully executed as a blasphemer and idolater. They subvert the Christian idea of Jesus' resurrection and insist that he got the punishment he deserved in hell—and that a similar fate awaits his followers."[92]

According to A. Steinsaltz, the Talmud is the most important book in Jewish culture, "the backbone of creativity and national life."[93] Peter Schäfer says that there is no doubt that the account of the execution of Jesus in the Talmud refers to Jesus of Nazareth, but states that the rabbinic literature in question is from a later Amoraic period, and may have drawn on the Christian gospels, or may have been created as a response to them.[94] A complete passage containing these contents is found in the Babylonian Sanhedrin 43a–b:

> On (Sabbath eve and) the eve of Passover Jesus the Nazarene was hanged and a herald went forth before him forty days heralding, "Jesus the Nazarene is going forth to be stoned because he practiced sorcery and instigated and seduced Israel to idolatry. Whoever knows anything in defense may come and state it." But since they did not find anything in his defense they hanged him on (Sabbath eve and) the eve of Passover. Ulla said: Do you suppose that Jesus the Nazarene was one for whom a defense could be made? He was a mesit (someone who instigated Israel to idolatry), concerning whom the Merciful [God] says: "Show him no compassion and do not shield him" (Deut. 13:9). With Jesus the Nazarene it was different. For he was close to the government.[95]

There are many unflattering references to Jesus dispersed throughout the Talmud. Schäfer explores "how the rabbis of the Talmud read, understood, and used the New Testament Jesus narrative to assert, ultimately, Judaism's superiority over Christianity—and how these stories divulge a notable familiarity with the Gospels—particularly Matthew and John—and represent a deliberate and sophisticated anti-Christian polemic that parodies the New Testament narratives."[96] This explicit animosity toward Jesus of Nazareth among his Jewish contemporaries corroborates his existence and historicity.

Second, the *Cambridge History of Latin Literature* asserts that the Roman historian and senator, Tacitus, makes a passing reference to Jesus, his execution by Pontius Pilate, and the existence of early Christians in Rome in his final work, *Annals* (written ca. AD 116), book 15, chapter 44.[97] According to Allen Brent, the *Annals* passage (15.44), which has been subjected to considerable scholarly inquiry, follows a description of the six-day Great Fire that burned much of Rome in July of AD 64.[98] The key part of the passage reads as follows:

> But all human efforts, all the lavish gifts of the emperor, and the propitiations of the gods, did not banish the sinister belief that the conflagration was the result of an order. Consequently, to get rid of the report, Nero fastened the guilt and inflicted the most exquisite tortures on a class hated for their abominations, called Christians by the populace. Christus, from whom the name had its origin, suffered the extreme penalty during the reign of Tiberius at the hands of one of our procurators, Pontius Pilatus, and a most mischievous superstition, thus checked for the moment, again broke out not only in Judæa, the first

source of the evil, but even in Rome, where all things hideous and shameful from every part of the world find their centre and become popular. Accordingly, an arrest was first made of all who pleaded guilty; then, upon their information, an immense multitude was convicted, not so much of the crime of firing the city, as of hatred against mankind.[99]

Allen Brent says Tacitus provides among the earliest non-Christian or Jewish references to the origins of Christianity, the execution of Christ depicted in the canonical gospels, and the presence and persecution of Christians in first century Rome.[100] According to Craig Evans, there is clear unanimity among scholars that Tacitus' passing reference to the execution of Jesus by Pontius Pilate is both genuine and possesses historic value as an unbiased and independent Roman source.[101]

Clearly, scholars perceive Tacitus' passing reference to Jesus, his execution by Pontius Pilate, and the existence of early Christians in Rome in 116 AD, as conclusive evidence of Jesus' historicity. Thus, it is indisputable that Jesus of Nazareth was a real historical figure rather than a mere abstraction or Christian invention—and that is the final straw that breaks the camel's back of skepticism about Jesus's historicity.

SOME SORT OF SUPER MAGNET

In the fall of 1984, the "Jesus Lectures," delivered by Jaroslav Pelikan, the Sterling Professor of History and Religious Studies at Yale, drew a thousand people who packed out the law school auditorium for weekly public lectures throughout the semester. Addressing "Jesus Through the Centuries," Pelikan provided observations and interpretations of Jesus as He has been seen through the ages, revealing ways He has influenced art, politics, music, literature and economics. One of the most notable quotes from Pelikan's Jesus lectures appeared in the *New York Times:*

> Regardless of what anyone may personally think or believe about him, Jesus of Nazareth has been the dominant figure in the history of Western Culture for almost 20 centuries. If it were possible, with some sort of super magnet, to pull up out of history every scrap of metal bearing at least a trace of his name, how much would be left?[102]

Almost forty years ago, this prolific Yale historian compared the pull Jesus has had on western civilization to some sort of super magnet. Was he right? What about today? Is the pull just as strong? Nick Spencer, a Cambridge social scientist and theologian asks the same question, "Why do we care? Why are we affected by the sight of the sacrificed Christ today? Why do we not share Nietzsche's hearty contempt for Christianity's 'slave morality,' his disdain for its founder's 'superficiality,' or his partiality for 'Olympus' over the 'crucified'? Why are we sympathetic to the cross?"[103] Spencer believes that the reason is because Jesus remade the ancient world like "some kind of metaphysical plague, which was pretty much what ancient and modern critics claim that it was" and its impact is still reverberating from the tree of glory.[104]

Simon Gathercole, in that poignant piece for the *Guardian* mentioned earlier, aptly concludes, "These abundant historical references leave us with little reasonable doubt that Jesus lived and died. The more interesting question—which goes beyond history and objective fact—is whether Jesus died and lived."[105]

REFLECTION QUESTIONS

1. Some argue that Jesus of Nazareth was doubly non-existent, suggesting that his existence is a mere hypothesis, that he is a Christian invention rather than a real historical figure. Have you ever heard this whispered on the grapevine by your friends or on social media?

2. Does reconstructing Jesus' life through critical historical methods (rather than a personal religious interpretation) give you confidence in his historicity?

3. Peter Schäfer says that there is no doubt that the account of the execution of Jesus in the Talmud refers to Jesus of Nazareth, but states that the rabbinic literature in question is from a later Amoraic period and may have drawn on the Christian gospels or been created as a response to them. Were you surprised to find Jesus in the Talmud?

4. In the fall of 1984, the "Jesus Lectures," delivered by Jaroslav Pelikan, drew a thousand people who packed out the law school auditorium throughout the semester. One of the most notable quotes from Pelikan's Jesus lectures appeared in the *New York Times*:

   "Regardless of what anyone may personally think or believe about him, Jesus of Nazareth has been the dominant figure in the history of Western Culture for almost 20 centuries. If it were possible, with some sort of super magnet, to pull up out of history every scrap of metal bearing at least a trace of his name, how much would be left?"

   How do you explain this dominant pull Jesus of Nazareth has had on Western culture for almost twenty centuries?

A PRAYER

Contemplating the uniqueness of Jesus:

"Regardless of what anyone may personally think or believe about him, Jesus of Nazareth has been the dominant figure in the history of Western Culture for almost 20 centuries. If it were possible, with some sort of super magnet, to pull up out of history every scrap of metal bearing at least a trace of his name, how much would be left?"[106]

Jaroslav Pelikan

Chapter 7

The Veracity Question: Is the New Testament *Reliable*?

"Christianity is not just an ethic; it's a historical event in which the kingdom of heaven invaded the realm of earth, in the great events of the incarnation, crucifixion and resurrection of Jesus the Christ."

F. F. Bruce

I recounted earlier how I once believed *Nightmare on Elm Street* was a biopic about Freddie Krueger, and that in the middle of junior high, I basically became a caffeine-dependent insomniac, convinced that Freddie was going to murder me in my sleep. This penchant for horror films—which have been proven to provoke psychological reactions and unnecessary and horrifying nightmares—has, unfortunately, somehow passed down to all my children. My wife insists that our two teen boys' love for the horror genre must be a genetic defect from my side of the family, since she has no such inclination. She's probably right, although when she's right, I usually only agree sarcastically—and that, too, is another unfortunate trait in our children she blames me for.

My youngest son collects vintage first edition Stephen King novels that have been adapted into blockbuster films. He is an eclectic kid; his favorite past-time on weekends is visiting vintage bookstores and thrift shops in search of overlooked classic gems. My oldest, on the other hand, has a deep curiosity about the occult and the paranormal, and watches the latest horror flicks spellbound in the dark. He is a gutsy kid. He wasn't scared of the dark at all when he was younger, and he is not scared of anything now really, except maybe for spiders...

Which is precisely why it came as a surprise when he came to my room in the middle of the night in a panic one time, asking for a prayer. He had had a terrible nightmare after watching the first episode of the Conjuring series. He couldn't shake off the feeling that something was wrong. Barely awake, I prayed for him, and then asked what it was about the episode that had disturbed him so. He said this one had hit so hard because it was based on a true story.

What story? I later learned that *The Conjuring* is based on a true story from 1971, and focuses on the Perrons, a family of seven who had moved into a farmhouse in Harrisville, Rhode Island. Paranormal investigators Ed and Lorraine Warren were called in to rid the house of its demonic presence, especially Bathsheba, "an accused witch who sacrificed her child to the devil and cursed future occupants of her home before killing herself."[107] But why does it matter? Is it not just entertainment at the end of the day? Why did the historicity of the events in this episode weigh so much more heavily on my son than the dozens of similar films he has watched before?

In a loosely parallel case, a similar question about historicity was raised by some within the church in the mid-1940s, when the reliability of the New Testament as a historical source (particularly the canonical gospels) was being disputed by modern scholarship. People were questioning if veracity of the New Testament as a record of historical facts really mattered. Surely the fundamental principles of Christianity are embedded in the Sermon on the Mount and other substrates in the New Testament? Why should the validity of those Scriptures be affected by the reality, or otherwise, of the historical framework, in which they are located?[108]

Does historicity matter? It does, of course, if something is to be taken seriously. It is easy to dismiss an eerie psychological reaction to a story as nothing more than an overactive imagination, unless it is based on a true story and grounded in an actual historical phenomenon. For then it is repeatable. This is ultimately what my son feared after watching the movie—that something similar could also happen to him. This is also the reason those in the broader culture in the late 1940s and today simply don't take Christianity seriously, or even dismiss it altogether. If Christianity is merely inspiring folklore, why would anyone need to dwell on it further, except as for casual entertainment?

WHY THE HISTORICITY OF THE NEW TESTAMENT MATTERS

According to N.T Wright, a prolific and leading Oxford historian of ancient antiquity, a growing chorus in church circles in the late 1940s suggested that history itself was irrelevant and possibly even damaging to faith. This was the type of talk that emboldened those in the broader culture and the academy to become more audacious in their critique of Christianity. It also explains why some historians have refuted the veracity of Christianity altogether.

> Can we trust the New Testament? Hasn't it all been disproved? Doesn't modern scholarship show that it was all made up much later, so that the supposedly historical foundations of Christianity are in fact a figment of the imagination? This sort of thing is said so often in the media, in some churches, and in public life in general that many people take it for granted that nothing can be said on the other side.[109]

Nonetheless, this assumption completely goes against the Apostle Paul's contention in 1 Corinthians 15 concerning the bodily resurrection of Jesus and how its historicity is of paramount importance to establishing the truth of the gospel. The aim of the gospel isn't to redefine how we look at the world philosophically, or even epistemologically. The purpose is to rearrange the way the world is ordered as a direct consequence of the resurrection, to reconstruct reality itself. Consequently, the way we see the world does change, not as a direct aim of the gospel message, but rather as a consequence. Paul argues that if we only have hope in Christ for this life, "we are, of all people, most to be pitied" (1 Cor. 15:19, NIV). In short, in contrast to those who suggest that the gospel's legitimacy is not affected by history, a view he considers hogwash, Paul contends that the very foundation of the gospel message is built upon the historicity of Jesus' life, death, and resurrection. In short, the truth of the gospel message and its historical basis are inseparable—and by extension the reliability of the New Testament as a historical source.

The late F. F. Bruce, a prolific historian and scholar who led the charge in upholding the historicity of the New Testament Canon during this controversial period, notes that some have erroneously contended that the veracity of the New Testament as a historical source doesn't matter if the fundamental principles of Christianity are embedded in the Sermon on the Mount and in other passages in the New Testament. He argues that it does matter if we can't know anything certain about the Teacher to whom these teachings are attributed. For if the story of Jesus as it has come down to us is myth or legend, and if it is the teaching ascribed to him that is important, whether Jesus was responsible or not, then "a man who accepts and follows that teaching can be a true Christian, even if he believes that Christ never lived at all." Bruce then says that this sort of argument may be applicable to some religions, but not to Christianity. He writes:

It might be held, for example, that the ethics of Confucianism have an independent value quite apart from the story of the life of Confucius himself, just as the philosophy of Plato must be considered on its own merits, quite apart from the traditions that have come down to us about the life of Plato and the question of the extent of his indebtedness to Socrates. But the argument can be applied to the New Testament only if we ignore the real essence of Christianity. For the Christian gospel is not primarily a code of ethics or a metaphysical system; it is first and foremost good news, and as such it was proclaimed by its earliest preachers. And this good news is intimately bound up with the historical order, for it tells how for the world's redemption God entered into history, the eternal came into time, the kingdom of heaven invaded the realm of earth, in the great events of the incarnation, crucifixion and resurrection of Jesus the Christ. The first recorded words of our Lord's public preaching in Galilee are: "The time is fulfilled, and the kingdom of God has drawn near; repent and believe the good news."[110]

Consequently, the veracity question is fundamental to the reliability of the New Testament as the closest historical source of Jesus' message in ancient antiquity. Granted, anyone who played "telephone" in elementary school knows that the message the teacher gives at the beginning is rarely the same message that reaches the end of the line. Often, the original message has changed into something entirely different by then. How, then, can the message of Jesus still be the same here and now after two thousand years? This is precisely why accepting both the reliability and the historicity of the New Testament as a historical record, and particularly the canonical gospels, is of paramount importance for establishing the legitimacy of the gospel message itself, since it contains the original message of Jesus. In short, can we prove the New Testament is reliable?

WHAT HISTORICAL RESEARCH REVEALS

To establish the New Testament as a legitimate historical source, this chapter examines what historical research reveals about the reliability of the New Testament canon compared to other historical documents in ancient antiquity, ones that are more generally accepted by scholars. For now, the purpose is simply to establish the veracity of the New Testament and not its authority, for without upholding the former, the latter falls.

According to Bruce, "the grounds for accepting the New Testament as trustworthy compare very favorably with the grounds on which classical students accept the authenticity and credibility of many ancient documents."[111] At the same time, Bruce notes that it is appropriate to look at the foundational documents of the New Testament from the standpoint of historical criticism, since Christianity claims to be a historical revelation.[112] He adds that in his experience, "secular students were readier to entertain seriously the claims of the gospel if they were persuaded that its documentary sources were (contrary to much popular prejudice) historically respectable." This is also needed in today's post-Christian world, where church attendance is precipitously in decline, and the Bible has become for many just a collection of archaic fables from a bygone time.

What do we learn when we compare the New Testament's reliability with that of other ancient historical documents through the lens of historical criticism? In an instructive analogy, Jay-Z, a prolific recording artist in the Hip Hop genre, perhaps even better known as the husband of Beyonce Knowles, borrows iconic lines from Julius Caesar, an infamous Roman general from antiquity, in his 2004 Grammy winning song Numb/

Encore, produced in collaboration with Linkin Park: "I came, I saw and conquered" to illustrate his dominance as one of the greatest rappers of all time.

That powerful line is translated from *"Veni, vidi, vici,"* a Latin phrase widely ascribed to Julius Caesar, who, according to Appian, used it in a letter to the Roman Senate around 47 BC, after he had attained a swift victory in his brief war against Pharnaces II of Pontus at the Battle of Zela. The maxim refers to a swift, decisive victory.[113]

Yet, when examining the meteoric rise and fall of Julius Caesar through the crucible of historical criticism, the earliest historical documents containing details of his life and deeds are few and far between. This pattern is also repeated in most major historical works of ancient antiquity. Professor F. F. Bruce, in his work entitled *The New Testament Documents: Are They Reliable*, fastidiously examines the historicity of almost all the major historical works in ancient antiquity, taking careful stock of when they were composed, the remaining legible copies, and the time lapse between the works and the events:[114]

1. For Caesar's *Gallic Wars* (composed between 58 and 50 BC), there are some extant manuscripts, but only nine or ten are eligible, and the oldest dates to some 950 years later than Caesar's day.

2. Of the 142 books of the *Roman History* of Livy (59 BC-AD 17), only thirty-five survived; these are recognized from no more than twenty manuscripts of any significance, only one of which, comprising portions of Books 3-6, is from the fourth century.

3. Of the fourteen books of the *Histories of Tacitus* (c. AD 100), only four and a half survive; of the sixteen books of his *Annals*, ten endure in full and two in part. The text of these extant portions of his two great historical works centers utterly on two documents, one from the ninth century and one from the eleventh. The extant manuscripts of his minor works (*Dialogus de Oratoribus, Agricola, Germania*) all originate from a codex of the tenth century.

4. The *History of Thucydides* (c. 460-400 BC) is known to us from eight manuscripts, the earliest from c. AD 900, and a few papyrus fragments dating to about the start of the Christian age. The same is true for the *History of Herodotus* (c. 488-428 BC). Yet, no classical scholar would contend that the existence of Herodotus or Thucydides is in question solely because the early manuscripts of their works that are of any use to us are more than 1,300 years older than the originals.

WHY THE NEW TESTAMENT STANDS ALONE AS A HISTORICAL SOURCE

What then do we learn when we compare the New Testament to other historical works in ancient antiquity through the lens of historical criticism? F. J. A. Hort, a Cambridge scholar specializing in ancient Greek and textual criticism, writes, "In the variety and fullness of the evidence on which it rests, the text of the New Testament stands absolutely and unapproachably alone among ancient prose writings."[115]

First, the New Testament was written somewhere between AD 40-100. The full manuscripts and their earliest copies range from AD 130 to AD 350. Thus, the longest time span between the earliest copies and their composition is anywhere between 30 to 250 years. Thus, through the lens of historical criticism, when the New Testament is compared to Caesar's *Gallic Wars,* for example, where the oldest copy was written some 950 years after Caesar's day, the New Testament documents are almost four times more reliable.

Second, there are well over 5,000 and 10,000 good legible copies of the New Testament in Greek and Latin, respectively, in tandem with 9,300 other manuscripts in fragments and other languages. Again, when comparing the remaining copies of Caesar's *Gallic Wars,* which only has nine surviving copies, to the New Testament, the latter is then 24,291 more reliable. Yes, that is not a typo; you read that correctly. Twenty-four thousand, two hundred and ninety-one! Professor Bruce concludes, "the evidence for our New Testament writings is ever so much greater than the evidence for many writings of classical authors, the authenticity of which no one dreams of questioning. And, if the New Testament were a collection of secular writings, their authenticity would generally be regarded as beyond all doubt."[116]

WHO IS THIS MAN?

We have already established that there is broad unanimity among biblical scholars and classical historians of ancient antiquity supporting the existence of Jesus of Nazareth as a Palestinian Jew who lived under the sovereignty of Tiberius Caesar Augustus, ruler of the Roman Empire from 14 AD to 37 AD. Thus, the science of historical criticism conclusively repudiates the erroneous claim that Jesus of Nazareth was a mere hypothesis or a figment of the Christian imagination. In addition, we have established how the veracity of the gospel message hinges on the flow of history, and by extension, the New Testament's reliability as a historical source, which we've proven conclusively in this chapter.

What then is left? As mentioned previously, Simon Gathercole, Professor of Early Christianity at Cambridge, in a piece for the *Guardian*, aptly concludes, "These abundant historical references leave us with little reasonable doubt that Jesus lived and died. The more interesting question—which goes beyond history and objective fact—is whether Jesus died and lived."[117] What then does the New Testament say about this? It says precisely that. Eyewitnesses testify that Jesus did, in fact, die and live, which does move the argument beyond history and objective fact.

However, history is itself quickly and easily forgotten, and leaving a mark on history is even more difficult. Yet, somehow, Jesus of Nazareth managed to completely avoid being forgotten for more than two millennia, and has managed instead to leave a mark that remains unrivalled. If contrast is the mother of clarity, we might compare Jesus to his most renowned contemporary, Tiberius Caesar Augustus, the emperor of Rome (even considered a god by the Romans). Tiberius, and indeed the other Caesars, are only invoked today when we describe a certain kind of salad dressing or a pizza from a similarly named outlet. By contrast, more than two billion people worship Jesus of Nazareth as king of all kings and the creator of the cosmos.

To put this incredible phenomenon into its proper context, consider this: The total global population in the first century was 170 million people. This means that Jesus of Nazareth today is not only remembered or revered by two billion followers, but worshipped as the exact representation of God by more than twelve times the entire global population of his own lifetime![118] Although historians fastidiously study history, most forget it. How then has this penniless Palestinian Jewish rabbi, who was crucified by the Roman empire for creating turmoil and disturbing the peace, become more famous today than in his time, if he didn't die and live?

This is the reason I often ask the most ardent skeptics if they have at least read the gospels for themselves before making a determination about the most predominant and central figure in all of history. More often than not, the answer is, "No I haven't. Who really has the time?" Not only is this lazy; it is also intellectually dishonest. I cannot emphasis enough how important it is to read the gospels before forming an opinion about who Jesus is, or whether he in fact died and lived.

C. S. Lewis, grappling with the gravity and weight of Jesus of Nazareth in history, argues that a man that said the sort of things Jesus said should not be considered a great moral teacher. He would be God's Son, an insane lunatic, or even the Devil himself. Lewis aptly concludes: "You must make your choice. Either this man was, and is, the Son of God: or else a madman or something worse. But let us not come with any patronizing nonsense about His being a great human teacher. He has not left that open to us. He did not intend to."[119]

REFLECTION QUESTIONS

1. When the reliability of the New Testament as a historical source was being disputed by modern scholarship, people were asking if it really mattered. Surely the fundamental principles of Christianity are embedded in the Sermon on the Mount and similar places in the New Testament? Why should the validity of those Scriptures be affected by the reality or otherwise of the historical framework in which they are located? What do you think?

2. Does the veracity of New Testament as a historical source matter, and if so why?

3. When the New Testament is compared to Caesar's *Gallic Wars,* the oldest copy of the latter was written some 950 years after Caesar's day, hence the New Testament documents are almost four times more reliable. Then, when comparing the remaining copies of Caesar's *Gallic Wars* (only nine) to the New Testament, statistically speaking the latter becomes 24,291 more reliable. Do those facts surprise you?

4. When we compare Jesus to his most renowned contemporary, Tiberius Caesar Augustus, the emperor of Rome (even considered a god by the Romans), we note Tiberius, and indeed the other Caesars, are only invoked today when we describe a certain kind of salad dressing or a pizza from a similarly-named outlet. By contrast, more than two billion people worship Jesus of Nazareth as king of all kings and the creator of the cosmos. How did a penniless Palestinian Jewish rabbi who was crucified by the Roman empire for creating turmoil and disturbing the peace become more famous today than in his time, if he didn't die and then live again?

A PRAYER

Grappling with the gravity and weight of Jesus of Nazareth in history.

"A man that said the sort of things Jesus said should not be considered a great moral teacher. He would either be God's Son or an insane lunatic or even the Devil himself. You must make your choice. Either this man was, and is, the Son of God: or else a madman or something worse. But let us not come with any patronizing nonsense about His being a great human teacher. He has not left that open to us. He did not intend to."

C. S. Lewis, *Mere Christianity*

Chapter 8

The Paranormal Question: Does God Still Speak Today?

"If we will listen, a sacred romance calls to us through our heart every moment of our lives. We've heard it in our favorite music, sensed it at the birth of our first child, been drawn to it while watching the shimmer of a sunset on the ocean. Something calls to us through experiences like these and rouses an inconsolable longing deep within our heart, and the voice that calls to us in this place is none other than the voice of God."
John Eldredge and Brent Curtis

On New Year's Eve, Andrew and Starbeth were dreaming of a beautiful outdoor May wedding overlooking the Hudson. They specifically asked me to officiate at their ceremony during sundown, so they and their guests would see the sun gradually descending toward the water at the beginning of the procession. "I hope it doesn't rain," I replied with a grin, and Andrew laughed nervously.

In hindsight, it is ironic to think that a little spring rain was the worst we feared when a global pandemic was looming. Little did we know that New York City would soon become the epicenter of the novel COVID-19 outbreak; that hospital tents would be pitched across Central Park; and that a naval fleet would tie up in New York Harbor to replenish the city's dwindling resources a month before the wedding. Starbeth's dream wedding quickly turned from a cute, quirky musical in La La Land, to a dystopian apocalypse in Zombieland.

Simone Weil, the late French philosopher, once wrote, "There are only two things that can pierce the human heart. One is beauty. The other is affliction."[120] In the modern age, most of us seek to avoid the latter at all costs, and hope only for the former. Yet, perhaps there is a certain poignant beauty found in affliction also, something we are missing, and that only an event as radical as a pandemic can teach us.

As the city shuttered and social distancing protocols were put into place, we knew a wedding cancellation was inevitable. We discussed alternatives, but rescheduling proved difficult, because Starbeth was an essential healthcare worker serving on the frontline at the peak of the outbreak. We decided that moving the ceremony forward was the best option, and that it would be best to hold the reception at a later date, when doing the Macarena wouldn't be such a criminal act (although our dance moves might be).

After finding some solace in finalizing a date, Starbeth was reminded of a dream that her friend Hailey had last spring. In the dream, Starbeth was downcast after Andrew proposed to her with a Teenage Mutant Ninja Turtle ring pop, when she was expecting the opening scene from *Breakfast at Tiffany's*. Nevertheless, with hindsight she now found it consoling. She felt God had sent her the dream, not as a foreshadowing of the pandemic per se, but rather as a silver lining in the thick of it.

The paranormal question concerns whether in fact God still speaks today. In the Christian tradition, although we believe God speaks primarily through his word (the Bible), God can also speak prophetically in a variety of ways, including film, art, music and even dreams. Brent Curtis and John Eldredge frame it this way in *The Sacred Romance*:

> If we will listen, a sacred romance calls to us through our heart every moment of our lives. It whispers to us on the wind, invites us through the laughter of good friends, reaches out to us through the touch of someone we love. Something calls to us through experiences like these and rouses an inconsolable longing deep within our heart, and the voice that calls to us in this place is none other than the voice of God.[121]

Yet, how can we be certain that it is actually God who is speaking, and not just our own imagination? How might we distinguish between a sign from God, and mere coincidence? When people in our culture today hear the word "prophecy," they immediately think of someone like Nostradamus foretelling future events, whereas the New Testament in fact frames prophecy primarily as *forthtelling* in and for the present moment. This is not to discount foretelling in any way, for the Old Testament does foreshadow the advent of Christ in numerous accounts. In fact, according to Nicky Gumbel, "Jesus fulfilled over 300 prophecies (spoken by different voices over 500 years), including twenty-nine major prophecies fulfilled in a single day—the day He died."[122] Yet the Pauline understanding of the main function of prophecy is not at all mystical, but is instead deeply practical. The aim of prophecy is primarily to lift others up and encourage them in their struggles, to free those who are prisoners of the moment here and now from doubting in the darkness what God said in the light.

In the spring of 2020, my spirits lifted greatly, as Andrew and Starbeth joined together in holy matrimony and exchanged their vows and Teenage Mutant Ninja Turtle ring pops. I began to better understand what Simone Weil meant by the exquisite confluence of beauty and affliction. Granted, this wasn't the hallmark wedding they had dreamt of. But somehow, through divine serendipity, they found their reality even better than the fantasy. You couldn't ask for any more from a wedding day. God had given them a day they will always remember and an epic tale to tell their grandchildren.

Ironically, it did rain on the day of the ceremony, but it didn't dampen our spirits. If anything, it felt like an ionic scene straight out of a Nicholas Sparks' romance novel; a sacred romance, the levity of Ninja Turtle ring pops and the jollity of holy laughter in the epoch of the coronavirus, all foreshadowed by a dream.

SERENDIPITY AS A SIGNPOST TO GOD'S HANDIWORK

I've mentioned previously that during the height of the COVID-19 pandemic, a few students who had recently started attending

Columbia University, and who were wrestling with their faith, asked individually if we could set up Zoom meetings to sort out a few things. When I finally met with Dylan over Zoom, I could tell he was deeply torn. He said that he wasn't yet quite sure, but probably wasn't a Christian anymore, and didn't know how to tell his parents. The very thought of breaking it to his parents was eating away at him more and more each day. Dylan's unbosoming, which was filled with so much ambivalence, told me everything and more about the burden he was carrying.

Yet, at same time, the fact that we were even having a conversation about faith was an act of divine serendipity. Dylan had no intention of attending a church after coming to New York. In fact, he came to New York to escape church. He said that he was really looking forward to sleeping in on weekends, skipping church and trying the latest brunch spots with friends, or even better, perhaps with a girlfriend. How then did Dylan end up at church if he was dead against it? Well, to cut a long story short, I guess you could say he bumped into us by mistake, or God had him bump into us on purpose. Come to think of it, perhaps it was a confluence of both. As the book of Proverbs says, although "we can make our plans, the LORD determines our steps" (Prov. 16:9, NLT).

On his first weekend away from Houston, Dylan was on his way to a gathering Columbia was hosting for new students on his program at Central Park. Coincidentally, our church was holding an outdoor Sunday service on the Upper West Side of Manhattan, adjacent to the Columbia meeting. Dylan ironically mistook our gathering for his, but soon discovered that we were actually a church. This could simply have been the end of the story, had not one of the first people he met at our church been another

Asian American Houstonian, called Tuna, who also recently started attending 180, and who, to his amazement, shared a close mutual friend of his back at home.

After bumping into us in the park, the more Dylan thought about it, the more confounded and confused he became. How was it that on the very Sunday he deliberately chose not to go to church, somehow the church came to him? Or was it actually the other way around—did he somehow mistakenly go to church? Was this mere coincidence or an act of divine serendipity?

If the former, then great. That was already the direction he was moving in, and with a willful blindness he could simply move on, leaving this archaic and constraining construct behind him. He could find a more sophisticated way of spending a Sunday afternoon, like brunching with friends on Eggs Benedict with a Mimosa in hand. If the latter, however, and an act of divine intervention, it would be both highly inconvenient and confounding to find God pursuing him, especially since one of the reasons he came to New York was to escape faith and his "very devoted Christian parents" breathing down his neck.

After attending church through till the end of the semester, Dylan got busy with school and volunteering at the UN and other related advocacy work, and his appearances at 180 became spotty and irregular. Then, out of the blue, I received a text on Facebook Messenger. Dylan was saying he could no longer ignore the hand of God in his life. I was intrigued and so I asked what had happened. The conversation went something like this:

Dylan: Do you know Cecily Pang? (*A Columbia graduate student pursuing a degree in Political Science.*)

Me: Yeah, she just recently started attending 180. Why?

Dylan: Call it case #48583838 of the serendipity of Dylan and 180, but she's my partner in one of the courses I'm taking this semester. *(Apparently she asked if he went to church and invited him to come to 180 with her.)*

Me: Talk about serendipity!

Dylan: It's getting a little too ridiculous to ignore now.

Me: Lol. God is pursing you in a way you might value.

Me: Come home.

Dylan: Given this new circumstance, I may be around two Sundays from now.

Me: Well, see you then! Tuna is getting baptized on the 21st.

Dylan: I have to be there!

Now, Dylan would be the first to tell you that he doesn't have this faith thing all figured out quite yet, or if he is ready to completely surrender his life to God. However, he knows that God's presence is real and moving in his life, and directionally he is moving closer and closer to where God is each day.

JESUS CALLING FROM ITHACA TO NEW YORK

I previously mentioned that during her freshman year at Cornell, a young woman named Rory was invited by a friend to attend a gathering on campus hosted by Intervarsity. As everyone lifted their voices and sang songs to God, she experienced a beauty and transcendence she had never felt before. She felt deeply affected by the gathering, because something so genuine about it touched almost every thread of her agnostic sense of life. At the same time, she also felt an immense discomfort, loneliness, and the poignant feeling that she didn't belong. Like Dorothy in the *Wizard of OZ*, she knew she wasn't in Kansas anymore, but the haunting was so overwhelming that she decided to leave that semester and never return. Nevertheless, four years later, and somewhat to her surprise, Rory found herself sitting in the pews of a church in New York, out of place, still grappling and haunted by what she had experienced in Ithaca.

Even she couldn't explain this poignant and evocative longing that kept gnawing at her heart. She eventually chalked it up to some unfinished business in college and a chapter she was ready to close, and in some ways went to church looking to self-sabotage her own spiritual journey and put an end this confounding haunting she couldn't control. Although she went to church much like one might go to dissect frogs in a laboratory, to her surprise, the very opposite happened. She developed many unexpected friendships, and learned much about God from people who really cared about her and her story, and from people who genuinely cared about God. Two years passed, and after arguing with friends in her small group about faith and asking a zillion questions during Bible studies, God's presence began to permeate the deepest parts of her heart, and she believed.

There was still a temptation to give in to a willful blindness and remain in control. This was not something she wanted to admit to anyone else or even to herself, because she knew what usually followed after such a declaration, and she wasn't quite ready. Taking the plunge and fully surrendering her life to God felt deeply frightening and something she might never be able to do. Then one day God prompted someone she deeply trusted (my wife!) to have a conversation with her about where she was with God. Rory knew deep down in her heart that while she denied it time and time again, from that night at Ithaca to this very moment, the voice calling out to her had always been Jesus, and somehow she knew on this very night in conversation with her Pastor that, it was now or never, and so she took the plunge and gave her life to Christ. These are Rory's own words on the day of her baptism:

> On November 11 of last year, I was speaking to my Pastor (Lydia), who had been praying for me for a while with many of the other people in my community. She sat me down and we talked. She just asked me what God was saying to me, and initially I had a great answer to sidetrack her, but I think there was part of me that had known God for a long time. I told her about the knowing in my heart that knew God's character—that he is kind, unchanging, perfect and true. It was a knowing that came after many years of arguing with people, hearing their stories, talking to myself, talking to God, and all of these things culminated in a sense of knowing. It was a knowing that I hid from people because of my fears.

With tears streaming down her face, Rory said that she didn't understand for the longest time why the disciples couldn't recognize Jesus when he appeared, because he was present in flesh.

But she then realized she almost didn't recognize him either. And how scary it is in hindsight to realize how close she came to missing him.

As the expression goes in the iconic song by the Beatles, the journey of faith is a "long and winding road" and not a straight path. Faith isn't monolithic or one-size-fits-all. It isn't linear, but is sinuous. Sometimes it gets worse before it gets better. God is a great artist. The Bible tells us he is painting a masterpiece and we are his canvas; except, he isn't finished yet. Thus, we might not be able to connect the dots in our lives just yet, since the dots often only make sense in reverse.

Sometimes God uses serendipity as a signpost to his presence working in someone's life, and other times his still small voice, as John Eldredge reminds us, "whispers to us on the wind, invites us through the laughter of good friends, and reaches out to us through the touch of someone we love."[123] In hindsight, if I've learned anything these last few years, it is that God is always speaking to us every moment of our lives. It is not that he isn't speaking; we just may not be listening. Perhaps this very moment is as good a time as any to start.

MIRACULOUS SIGNS

I shared previously that while in college I plunged into a crisis, and even before I knew it, I was navigating the darkest spiritual period I had ever known. The more I questioned, the more unsure I became, and the deeper I sank into despair. One day I decided to take the garbage out of my dorm room, which in itself was kind of a miracle, because I seldom did. I murmured while walking down the stairs, "God, if you exist, make it snow and I will believe." And I am telling you, my wife remembers this day as well, for with no exaggeration, a few minutes after I mumbled my prayer in the middle of April, it began to snow.

I still remember my wife (we were just friends then) asking me, "Why is it snowing in the middle of spring?" Of course, she had no idea I was praying for a sign. As I stepped outside and saw the snowfall, you'd think I would have fallen on my face on the ground, like Thomas after feeling the scars on Jesus' hands and feet, and cried out, "My lord and my God!"

People have completely surrendered to God after much less, but my response was surprisingly non-committal for someone who had witnessed a miracle. "It's just a coincidence," I scoffed, and proceeded to throw out the trash and go back inside as if nothing had happened.

I now recognize that God answered my prayer and gave me the very miraculous sign I asked for, and I cringe at my own sinful stubbornness. For I still didn't believe. In hindsight, I realize that there are different degrees of "willful blindness" in all of us that directly resist God's work in our lives. Some have described this inner resistance as the pride of the flesh—the very sin that sunk the devil—and others the fear of losing control. But whatever you call it, it is an immunity that resists the work of God's Spirit. Many, limited by their naturalistic worldview, lose sight of the fact that faith is also interwoven with a spiritual battle that is usually hidden in plain sight. This is why the last question I always ask during a baptism ceremony is, "Do you hereby renounce, repudiate and reject the kingdom of darkness, and Satan and all his works with all his pomp and pride?"[124] For the last line of defense before surrendering fully into God's hand is to surrender the sin of pride and willful blindness.

In many ways, I now realize that it was far easier for God to remove the stone that was guarding Jesus' tomb than the pride guarding my own heart. For the former could not resist, but the latter can. Miracles in themselves cannot resolve all the doubts or produce faith in the way that many assume. A miracle did not do so for me, nor did it do so for the disciples. I know Thomas adamantly declared that he would only believe if he felt Jesus' hands and feet, but Jesus complying with his request wasn't a miracle; it was instead an act of love.

Thus, miraculous signs can only accomplish in hindsight what they could not do in the present: they provide proof that God loves us, even while we are still sinners. I realize now that God didn't make it snow in April so I could believe, but rather that I might realize in hindsight that I was loved. For me, it took something even greater than a miracle to remove the stone that was guarding my heart: his unconditional love.

As Terence, the Roman playwright, once wrote, "The more we wish the less we believe." How many signs will it take before we simply attribute them to mere coincidence again? How many sunsets and sunrises before we explain the beauty away with a scientific explanation? My advice to anyone sincerely looking for God is this: Don't pray for signs; pray rather that somehow you begin to understand his love for you. Ultimately that is the only force that is strong enough in the universe to tame your willful blindness. For only perfect love can cast out fear.

REFLECTION QUESTIONS

1. The paranormal question concerns whether in fact God still speaks today. In the Christian tradition, although we believe God speaks primarily through his word (the Bible), God can also speak prophetically in a variety of ways, including film, art, music and in dreams. Have you ever experienced or sensed God was speaking through a scene in a film or music?

2. After bumping into our Church in the park, the more Dylan thought about it, the more confounded and confused he became. How was is that on the very Sunday he deliberately chose not to go to church, somehow the church came to him? Or was it actually the other way around—did he somehow mistakenly go to church? Was this mere coincidence or an act of divine serendipity?

3. What do you take away from Dylan's story at the park? Could serendipity be a signpost to God's handiwork in someone's life? How can we be certain that it is God who is speaking and not just our imagination? How might we distinguish between a sign from God and mere coincidence? What about Dylan being paired with Cecily Pang for a project in class at Columbia? Would you categorize that as divine serendipity?

4. I now recognize that God answered my prayer and gave me the very miraculous sign (snowfall) I asked for and I cringe at my own sinful stubbornness. For I still didn't believe. In hindsight, I realize that there are different degrees of "willful blindness" in all of us that directly resist God's work in our lives.

What kind of resistance, either internal ("willful blindness") or external (spiritual warfare) have you experienced in your own faith journey?

A PRAYER

"You will seek me and find me when you seek me with all your heart."

Jeremiah 29:13, NIV.

"We should not cease from exploration and at the end of all our exploring we will arrive at the place we started and know the place for the first time."

T. S. Eliot, Four Quartets.

Conclusion

"I stand at the door and knock."
Revelation 3:20 (NIV)

NEXT STEPS

onfession: my intention is not to convert anyone, but rather to help bring to the surface what might already be brewing beneath. My hope is to start a genuine dialogue about things that really matter and that touch the deepest parts of our lives—the things we often ponder about in the middle of the night when we are least guarded and most vulnerable. It is in those moments we feel a holy haunting that is quite hard to describe, but which is nevertheless evocative and difficult to ignore.

My hope is to help you get close enough to see for yourself what might lie beyond the horizon. I've already stated my position quite clearly in the introduction. My hope is that after weighing the evidence, you will reframe your notion of faith from a leap to something more judicious, or as Anne Lamott puts it in *Traveling Mercies*, to see crossing the swamp of doubt and fear "not as a leap, but rather as a series of staggers from what seems like one safe place to another."[125] Perhaps my musings and candor about my own struggles with the swamp might help you. That is my genuine hope and prayer.

CROSSING THE SWAMP

Crossing the swamp is never an easy task. Bear Grylls, the former British special forces member turned TV adventurer, made it look sexy on TV, but I seriously doubt he enjoyed it, not even once in his six seasons on *Man vs Wild*. In the swamp, you aren't greeted by cute gators like the ones on some yuppie's polo, but by a congregation of ravening beasts crying "YOLO." Honestly, even the word swamp evokes unpleasant feelings, so just imagine the resistance you'd feel to realize the only way across was to jump in with both feet while holding your nose!

I once had a fashionista on the day of her baptism refuse to wear a T-shirt commemorating the day because it violated her sense of fashion. Coming to faith may not be a leap, but it's no cakewalk either. Sometimes, you will have to take off the Dolce & Gabbana and don a tacky T-Shirt and get wet. Although she eventually reluctantly agreed, I have no idea what she was even complaining about, because I am like a good Methodist at heart: I never dunk, I only sprinkle.

As previously mentioned, Rory too felt that reluctance to cross the swamp. After two years of arguing with friends in her small group about faith and asking a zillion questions during Bible studies, God's presence began to permeate the deepest parts of her heart, and she believed. Yet, there was still very much a temptation to give in to willful blindness and remain in control. This was not something she wanted to admit to anyone else, or even to herself, because she knew what usually followed after such a declaration, and she wasn't quite ready.

Perhaps after reading this book, like Rory, you have come to believe as well, yet fully surrendering your life to God feels deeply frightening and something you may never be able to do. Still, you know deep down that, although you may have denied it time and time again, the voice calling out to you both in the past and at this very moment is, and always has been, the voice of God. Is it possible to finally give in to God, even while still dragging your feet?

In *Surprised by Joy*, C. S. Lewis tells a very personal and vulnerable story about the night he finally fully surrendered his life to Christ, describing himself as the most dejected and reluctant convert in all of England. Although he initially felt hesitant, in hindsight, he was "surprised by joy" because he discovered that the "hardness of God is kinder than the softness of men, and His compulsion is our liberation."[126] Lewis recalls his coming to faith moment with great nostalgia, as he writes:

> The odd thing was that before God closed in on me, I was in fact offered what now appears a moment of wholly free choice. In a sense. I was going up Headington Hill on the top of a bus. Without words and (I think) almost without images, a fact about myself was somehow presented to me. I became aware that I was holding something at bay, or shutting something out. Or, if you like, that I was wearing some

stiff clothing, like corsets, or even a suit of armour, as if I were a lobster. I felt myself being, there and then, given a free choice. I could open the door or keep it shut; I could unbuckle the armour or keep it on. Neither choice was presented as a duty; no threat or promise was attached to either, though I knew that to open the door or to take off the corset meant the incalculable. You must picture me alone in that room at Magdalen, night after night, feeling, whenever my mind lifted even for a second from my work, the steady, unrelenting approach of Him whom I so earnestly desired not to meet. That which I greatly feared had at last come upon me. In the Trinity Term of 1929 I gave in, and admitted that God was God, and knelt and prayed: perhaps, that night, the most dejected and reluctant convert in all England.[127]

Likewise, on the day of her baptism, with tears streaming down her face, Rory said that she didn't understand for the longest time why the disciples couldn't recognize Jesus when he appeared, present in the flesh. But she then realized she almost didn't recognize him either, and how scary it was in hindsight to realize how close she came to missing him. Yet, somehow, she knew on that very night in conversation with her pastor that it was now or never, and so she took the plunge and gave her life to Christ.

GIVING IN TO GOD

What then does it look like to finally give in to God? C. S. Lewis came to faith as the most dejected and reluctant convert in all of

England. Rory gave in to God while still dragging her feet. In short, there isn't an ideal or perfect way to come to faith. The point is to simply give in, no matter how reluctantly! The reluctance usually indicates an understanding of the gravity of the moment and the commitment that follows. This is itself a good indication that we know it's time and long overdue. It's time to come home. If this resonates with you, I want to invite you to just take a moment and pause in silence and reflection, and pray these words after me:

> Jesus, I believe you are the Son of God, that you died on the cross to rescue me from sin and death and to restore me to the Father. I choose now to turn from my sins, my self-centeredness, and every part of my life that does not please you. I choose you. I give myself to you. I receive your forgiveness and ask you to take your rightful place in my life as my Savior and Lord. Come reign in my heart, fill me with your love and your life, and help me to become a person who is truly loving—a person like you. Restore me, Jesus. Live in me. Love through me. Thank you, God. In Jesus' name I pray. Amen.[128]

If you have just prayed those words, I want to personally welcome you to God's family! Heaven is throwing a party right now celebrating your homecoming! I can't wait to meet you one day in this life or in eternity.

Yet, for some others, coming to faith may still feel a bit premature, and that is completely okay. I want to encourage you with the words of C. S. Lewis as he addresses the conundrum and the often messy complexities of one's faith journey:

> The world does not consist of 100 percent Christians and 100 percent non-Christians. There are people (a great many of them) who are slowly ceasing to be Christians but who still call themselves by that name: some of them are clergymen. There are other people who are slowly becoming Christians though they do not yet call themselves so. There are people who do not accept the full Christian doctrine about Christ but who are so strongly attracted by Him that they are His in a much deeper sense than they themselves understand.[129]

I would also encourage you to download the Bible App from YouVersion and the Jesus Calling App by Sarah Young, so that you might continue your conversation with God through daily Scripture reading, in tandem with short daily devotionals.

In addition, for those of us who grew up in the church, questioning the truth of Christianity can feel like a betrayal. I wish someone had told me at the start of my own struggle with faith in college that it is human to doubt, and that doubt feels a lot like fear. You see, I once believed that I had to walk through the valley of the shadow of death alone. I thought that was how apostasy worked. I couldn't have been more wrong. Not only was God with me in the darkness, but God was holding my hand, guiding me back home. I once believed that I had to walk through the darkness alone and afraid, but now I know that I never once walked alone, and you haven't either. He was beside you all along, even when you couldn't tell. Remember, faith was never meant to be lived alone. I want to encourage you to consider joining a local church near you and finding friends along the journey to share your life with.

Lastly, if you are a devoted believer, entering genuine gospel conversations with secular friends in the university and the public square presents a considerable challenge. And so this book was also written so that believers might seamlessly invite their friends to read along and sincerely investigate the claims of Jesus for themselves.

Would you pray with me in faith right now that the Holy Spirit will show you a few people in your life that could benefit from reading this book along with you? Just for a moment, would you lift your hands to God and pray these words out loud:

> "Holy Spirit, would you give me a few names or faces of people in my life who would benefit from reading this book along with me?"

Honestly, sharing Jesus to a hurting and broken world can sometimes sound almost like a cliché as we sip our espresso at Starbucks, while listening to the incredible Brook Ligertwood exhorting us to sing "a thousand hallelujahs and a thousand more."[130] Yet, the truth is, we probably agonize more over what specialty drink we should buy than over the faces of lost people across the street or in the Amazon.

Don't worry, I promise not to rant about the dangers of modern luxuries. I watch more TV than most pastors and I really like gourmet coffee. I lack the moral authority to judge anyone. Instead, I come alongside you as a friend on the journey, also desiring to love like Jesus in the age of avocado toast and Jamba juice.

KNOCKING ON HEAVEN'S DOOR

First impressions leave a distinct mark. MJ was collected, intelligent, and played the guitar and sang like Sarah McLachlan. It seemed her whole life was ahead of her, with the best yet to come. Yet, things are not always as they appear. The truth is, she couldn't get through a single day without getting high or drunk, or contemplating if she should end it all. This was really hard for me to accept, but that was the story she shared the day we baptized her in the heart of NYC.

MJ came to Christ through our campus ministry at NYU. The day she prayed to invite Christ into her life, she also quit drugs cold turkey. She said that, oddly, she felt no pull towards them anymore. However, the real kicker wouldn't come until a few months later, when our community was reminded once again of the all-surpassing greatness of the gospel in Christ! The topic of heaven came up in a Bible study, and MJ almost died of happiness, screaming: "Do you mean to say that I get to be with Jesus not just for this life, but forever? That is crazy!"

She squealed too many times to count and began to praise God. MJ was an international student from Japan, and Christianity was still very new to her. It had never dawned on us that she may not have heard of heaven! What most of us took for granted from Sunday School intoxicated her with such joy!

I'm learning that sharing Jesus to a hurting and broken world isn't plastic at all. There is nothing plastic about MJ's life and the lives of others like her. If anything, it is us who are plastic and the ones who need to come out of the safety of our bubble wrap and get real. I can't imagine what MJ was going through before she met Christ. Although I didn't know, heaven knew, and it haunts me a little more each time I reflect upon her story, and now I hope it haunts you too.

REFLECTION QUESTIONS

1. My hope is that after weighing the evidence you will reframe your notion of faith from a leap to something more judicious. At the end of this book where would you say you are in your own faith journey? (1) Ready to come to faith? (2) Ready, but dragging your feet? (3) Needing a little more time to process?

2. Coming to faith may not be a leap, but it's no cakewalk either. What are a few of the barriers that are preventing you from coming to faith?

3. On the day of her baptism, with tears streaming down her face, Rory said that she hadn't understood why the disciples couldn't recognize Jesus when He appeared in the flesh. But then she realized she almost didn't recognize Him either, and how scary it was in hindsight to realize how close she came to missing him. How about you, are you missing him, or are you seizing the day to come to faith, no matter how reluctantly?

4. Lastly, if you are already a devoted believer, entering genuine gospel conversations with secular friends in the university and the public square presents a considerable challenge. So would you pray with me in faith that the Holy Spirit will show you a few people in your life who would benefit from reading this book along with you? Things are not always as they appear, and could you be overlooking someone like MJ in your life right now?

PRAYER

C. S. Lewis on the night he came to faith:

The odd thing was that before God closed in on me, I was in fact offered what now appears a moment of wholly free choice. In a sense. I was going up Headington Hill on the top of a bus. Without words and (I think) almost without images, a fact about myself was somehow presented to me. I became aware that I was holding something at bay, or shutting something out. Or, if you like, that I was wearing some stiff clothing, like corsets, or even a suit of armour, as if I were a lobster.

I felt myself being, there and then, given a free choice. I could open the door or keep it shut; I could unbuckle the armour or keep it on. Neither choice was presented as a duty; no threat or promise was attached to either, though I knew that to open the door or to take off the corset meant the incalculable.

You must picture me alone in that room at Magdalen, night after night, feeling, whenever my mind lifted even for a second from my work, the steady, unrelenting approach of Him whom I so earnestly desired not to meet. That which I greatly feared had at last come upon me. In the Trinity Term of 1929 I gave in, and admitted that God was God, and knelt and prayed: perhaps, that night, the most dejected and reluctant convert in all England.[131]

C. S. Lewis, Surprised by Joy

About The Author

R ev. Dr. Sam D. Kim (DMIN; MDIV) is the Co-founder and Senior Minister of 180 Church near Union Square in Downtown Manhattan, with a congregation primarily made up of those in healthcare, engineering, and STEM related fields. Dr. Kim has been ministering to Christians in elite secular institutions who are studying or conducting groundbreaking research; to Christian physicians in multiple specialties flourishing in their work in the city, and to Christian engineers working at top tech companies seeking to solve the world's greatest problems.

He is a Harvard-trained ethicist and was appointed as a research fellow in Global Health and Social Medicine at Harvard Medical School Center for Bioethics and part of Harvard catalyst, where he explored the inequities surrounding health, immigration, and social policies. He is a recipient of a Lifelong Learning Fellowship at Yale Divinity School and Yale Medicine, which aims to close the gap between faith and science and is awarded by the John Templeton Foundation and AAAS. He is a regular contributor at *Christianity Today*, YouVersion at the Bible APP, Church Leaders at Outreach, and the Billy Graham Center at Wheaton College. He lives in New York City with his wife Lydia, and his two sons, Nathan and Josh.

Additional Resources

For more from Dr. Sam D. Kim

Please visit his website www.samdkim.com or www.aholyhauntingbook.com

Follow on Social

Instagram: Sammydkim

FB: drsammykim

Twitter @drsammykim

Share Good News with us!

If you came to faith and gave in to God while reading this book, please share the good news with us at goodnews@180church.tv

Looking for Community?

Remember faith was never meant to be lived alone. I strongly encourage you to join a local church near you. (If you need help finding a local church, please email find@180church.tv.)

Looking forLooking for a Church?

Catch Dr. Sam's sermons live on most Sundays @ 12:10 EST at www.180church.tv or directly on YouTube at www.youtube.com/user/180Churchnyc

Endnotes

1   C. S. Lewis, *Mere Christianity* (London: HarperCollins, 2007), Kindle edition, 208–209.

2   Robert Kegan, *The Evolving Self: The Problem and Process of Human Development* (Cambridge, MA: Harvard University Press, 1982), 107–109.

3   What is Evolutionary Creation?" available on the website of biologos.com.

4   Jon Bloom, "What Does 'Deconstruction' Even Mean?" February 15, 2022, available on the website of desiringgod.org.

5   Gary Aylesworth, "Postmodernism," *The Stanford Encyclopedia of Philosophy* (Spring 2015), Edward N. Zalta (ed.), available on the website of plato.stanford.edu.

6   Bloom, "What Does 'Deconstruction' Even Mean?"

7   Anne Lamott, *Traveling Mercies* (New York: Anchor Books, 1999), 3.

8   Peter Kreeft, and Ronald K. Tacelli, *Handbook of Christian Apologetics* (Downers Grove, IL: InterVarsity Press, 2009), 89.

9   Richard Dawkins, *The God Delusion* (New York: Houghton Mifflin, 2008), 161.

10   Francis S. Collins, *The Language of God* (New York: Simon & Schuster), Kindle Edition, 4.

11   Augustine, *The Confessions of St. Augustine* (New York: P. F. Collier & Son, 1909), 5.

12   David Brooks, "Fighting the Spiritual Void," *New York Times*, November 19, 2018.

13   Brooks, "Fighting the Spiritual Void."

14   Douglas Nemecek, "Cigna U.S. Loneliness Index. Survey of 20,000 Americans Examining Behaviors Driving Loneliness in the United States," (2018), 1–3.

15   Bob Dylan, *Chronicles*, Vol.1 (London: Simon & Schuster, 2011), 12.

16   Apparently, at times Bono snuck in to hear Darrell preach at Glendale Presbyterian Church near Hollywood. However, it wasn't until Darrell was a Professor at Regent College in Vancouver that he learned he was one of Bono's favorite preachers. Bono was in Vancouver for a concert and visited Regent's bookstore to get more of Darrell's sermons and left a note revealing all of this, and saying he was a big fan.

17   Darrell W. Johnson, *Experiencing the Trinity* (Vancouver: Regent College, 2002), 37.

18   T. S. Eliot, *Four Quartets* (Orlando, FL: Harcourt Books, 2014), 59.

19   See StarChild Question of the Month for Feb 2001 on the NASA's StarChild website.

20   Nemecek, "Cigna U.S. Loneliness Index," 2.

21 Lewis, *Mere Christianity*, 139.

22 Kayne West, "Runaway," retrieved from Apple.com. Released 2010.

23 C. H. Liu, C Stevens, S. H. M. Wong, M. Yasui, and J. A. Chen, "The Prevalence and Predictors of Mental Health Diagnoses and Suicide among U.S. College Students: Implications for Addressing Disparities in Service Use," *Depress Anxiety* 36 (2019): 8–17.

24 Minority students were found to be less likely to report all outcomes compared to white students. Another significant discovery was that LGBTQ students were most at risk of mental health disorders or self-injury, with two-thirds reporting self-injury and more than half struggling with suicidal ideation.

25 Liu, et al., "The Prevalence and Predictors of Mental Health Diagnoses," 8–17.

26 Steven Pinker, "How Humanity Gave Itself an Extra Life," *New York Times*, April 27, 2021.

27 Daniel G. Groody, *Globalization, Spirituality, and Justice*. Theology in Global Perspective (Maryknoll, NY: Orbis Books, 2015), 255.

28 Brent Curtis and John Eldredge, *The Sacred Romance: Drawing Closer to the Heart of God* (Nashville, TN: Thomas Nelson, 1997), 6–7.

29 G. K. Chesterton, *Orthodoxy* (London: John Lane, 1909), 110.

30 Kegan, *The Evolving Self*, 29.

31 Stephen R. Covey, *The 7 Habits of Highly Effective People* (Australia: Rosetta Books, 1989), Kindle Edition, 66.

32   Robert Kegan, *In Over Our Heads: The Mental Demands of Modern Life* (Cambridge, MA: Harvard University Press, 1994), 9.

33   Kegan, *The Evolving Self*, 107.

34   Kegan, *The Evolving Self*, 30.

35   Kegan, *The Evolving Self*, 107–109.

36   Kegan, *The Evolving Self*, 11.

37   Kegan, *The Evolving Self*, 41.

38   Kegan, *In Over Our Heads*, 45.

39   Kegan, *In Over Our Heads*, 44.

40   Kegan, *In Over Our Heads*, 7.

41   Kegan, *In Over Our Heads*, 7–8.

42   Kegan, *In Over Our Heads*, 45.

43   Brooks, "Fighting the Spiritual Void."

44   Augustine, *The Confessions*, 96.

45   Stephen Hawking, *A Brief History of Time* (London: Bantam Dell, 1998), 210.

46   Ronald H. Nash, *Faith and Reason: Searching for a Rational Faith* (Grand Rapids, MI: Zondervan, 1994), 80.

47   Kegan, *In Over Our Heads*, 1.

48   Donald, Miller, *A Million Miles in a Thousand Years: What I Learned While Editing My Life* (Nashville, TN: Thomas Nelson, 2009, 6.

49   C. S. Lewis, *The Complete C.S. Lewis* (San Francisco, CA: Harper San Francisco, 2008), 39.

50   Tim Keller, "Growing My Faith in The Face of Death," *The Atlantic*, March 2021.

51   Tish Harrison Warren, *Prayer in the Night* (Westmont, IL: InterVarsity Press, 2021), Kindle Edition, 12.

52   F. Newport, "Millennials' Religiosity Amidst the Rise of the Nones," August 30, 2020, Gallup.

53   Henri Nouwen, *You Are the Beloved: Daily Meditations for Spiritual Living* (New York: Crown, 2017), 326.

54   Frederick Buechner, *The Clown in the Belfry: Writings on Faith and Fiction*. San Francisco: HarperSanFrancisco, 1992, 172.

55   Horatio Spafford and composed by Philip Bliss, "It is well with my Soul." 1876.

56   David Brooks, "America is Having A Moral Convulsion," *The Atlantic*, October 2020.

57   "Church Membership falls Below Majority," Gallup.

58   Laura Miller, "The Da Vinci Con," *New York Times*, February 22, 2004.

59   Alister McGrath, "Deluded About God? A Reflection on Richard Dawkins' *The God Delusion*," C. S. Lewis Institute.

60   Dawkins, *The God Delusion*, 161.

61   Isaac Newton, *Isaaci Newtoni Opera quae exstant omnia* (London: John Nichols, nd), 436–437.

62   Collins, *The Language of God*, 20.

63   Collins, *The Language of God*, 16.

64   Timothy Keller, *The Reason for God: Belief in an Age of Skepticism* (New York: Penguin Publishing Group, 2008), xviii.

65   Mark Twain, *The Innocents Abroad* (New York: Chelsea House, 2021), 2: 407.

66   Jane Austen, *Pride and Prejudice* (New York: Little, Brown, 1906), 86.

67   Kenneth Chang, "Elon Musk's Plan: Get Human Beings to Mars and Beyond," *New York Times,* September 28, 2016.

68   C. S. Lewis, "Bluspels and Flalansferes: A Semantic Nightmare," in *Selected Literary Essays*, ed. Walter Hooper (Cambridge: Cambridge University Press, 1969), 265.

69   Chesterton, *Orthodoxy*, 110.

70   Bruce Marshall, *The World, the Flesh, and Father Smith* (Boston: Houghton Mifflin, 1945), 108.

71   "How is Evolutionary Creation different from Evolutionism, Intelligent Design, and Creationism?" Available on the website of biologos.com.

72   Mark McEntire, *Struggling with God: An Introduction to the Pentateuch* (Macon, GA: Mercer University Press, 2008), 8.

73   Archer L. Gleason, *Encyclopedia of Bible Difficulties* (Ada, MI: Baker, 1982), 60-61.

74   "What is Evolutionary Creation?"

75   T. S. Eliot, *Four Quartets* (Orlando, FL: Harcourt Books, 2014), 59.

76   R. Jastrow, *God and the Astronomers* (New York: W. W. Norton, 1992), 107.

77   See Francis Su, "Can Mathematics Be Spiritual? Ask Einstein," on the website of Big Think.

78   Andrew May, "What is the Big Bang Theory?" Available on the website of space.com.

79   Jonathan Lunine, "Faith and the Expanding Universe of Georges Lemaitre," *Church Life Journal*, 2019.

80 Lunine, "Faith and the Expanding Universe of Georges Lemaitre."

81 Collins, *The Language of God*, 5–6.

82 C. R. Darwin, *The Origin of Species* (New York: Penguin, 1958), 459.

83 Collins, *The Language of God*, 68.

84 "How could humans have evolved and still be in the "Image of God?" Biologos.com.

85 Darwin, *The Origin of Species*, 459.

86 "The World Bank in Kazakhstan, Economy at a Glance," available on the website of worldbank.org.

87 Simon Gathercole, "What is the Historical Evidence that Jesus Christ Lived and Died?" *The Guardian*, April 14, 2017.

88 Frank Leslie Cross and Elizabeth A. Livingstone, *The Oxford Dictionary of the Christian Church* (Oxford: Oxford University Press, 2005), 779.

89 B. D. Ehrman, *Forged: Writing in the Name of God* (New York: HarperOne, 2011), 4–5.

90 Graham Stanton, *The Gospels and Jesus,* Oxford Bible Series, 2nd ed. (Oxford: Oxford University Press, 2002), 145.

91 Robert E. van Voorst, *Jesus Outside the New Testament* (Grand Rapids, MI: Wm. B. Eerdmans 2000), 13.

92 Peter Schäfer, *Jesus in the Talmud* (Princeton, NJ: Princeton University Press, 2009).

93 Steinsaltz, A., and C. Galai, *The Essential Talmud,* 13th ed. (New York: Basic Books, 2009), 3

94 Schäfer, *Jesus in the Talmud*, 9, 17, 141.

95 Schäfer, *Jesus in the Talmud*, 64–65.

96 Description of "Jesus in the Talmud", available on the website of press.princeton.edu.

97 P. E. Easterling, and E. J. Kenney, eds., *The Cambridge History of Latin Literature* (Cambridge: Cambridge University Press, 1982), 892.

98 Allen Brent, *A Political History of Early Christianity* (Edinburgh: T&T Clark. 2009), 32–34.

99 Tacitus, *Annals*, ed. A. J. Church and W. J. Brodribb (Perseus, online edition), XV.

100 Brent, *A Political History of Early Christianity*, 32–34.

101 Craig A. Evans, *Jesus and His Contemporaries: Comparative Studies* (Leiden: Brill Publishers, 2001), 42.

102 Michael Luzzi, "A View of Jesus' Impact on Cultures," *New York Times*, December 1, 1985.
The full quotation is found in Jaroslav Pelikan, *Jesus Through the Centuries: His Place in the History of Culture* (London: Yale University Press, 1999), 1.

103 Tom Holland, *Revolutionary: Who was Jesus? Why Does He Still Matter?* (London: SPCK, 2020), 86.

104 Holland, *Revolutionary*, 86.

105 Gathercole, "What is the Historical Evidence?"

106 Michael Luzzi, "A View of Jesus' Impact on Cultures."

107 Emily Tannenbaum, Mehera Bonner and Adrianna Freeman, "The Conjuring True Story," *Cosmopolitan*, June 4, 2021.

108 F. F. Bruce, *The New Testament Documents: Are They Reliable?* (London: Kingsley Books), Kindle Edition, 6.

109 Bruce, *The New Testament Documents*, 3.

110 Bruce, *The New Testament Documents*, 6.

111 Bruce, *The New Testament Documents*, 3.

112 Bruce, *The New Testament Documents*, 4.

113 Clifford Ando, *Imperial Ideology and Provincial Loyalty in the Roman Empire* (Berkeley, CA: University of California Press, 2000), 389.

114 Bruce, *The New Testament Documents*, 13.

115 F. J. A. Hort, *The New Testament in the Original Greek*, Vol. I (London: Macmillan, 1956), 561.

116 Bruce, *The New Testament Documents*, 12.

117 Gathercole, "What is the Historical Evidence that Jesus Christ Lived and Died?"

118 Adam Frank, "200,000 Years of Holidays Where Do You Fit In?" December 20, 2016, available on the website of NPR.org.

119 Lewis, *Mere Christianity*, 52.

120 George A. Panichas, ed., *Simone Weil Reader* (Mt Kisco, NY: Moyer Bell, 1977), 421–422.

121 Curtis and Eldredge, *The Sacred Romance*, 6–7.

122 Nicky Gumbel, *Questions Of Life* (New York: Alpha North America, 2011), Kindle Edition, 424.

123 Curtis and Eldredge, *The Sacred Romance*, 6–7.

124 *The Pastor's Handbook NIV: Instructions, Forms and Helps for Conducting the Many Ceremonies a Minister is Called Upon to Direct* (Nashville, TN: Moody Publishers), Kindle Edition, 497.

125 Lamott, *Traveling Mercies*, 3.

126 C. S. Lewis, *Surprised by Joy: The Shape of My Early Life* (New York: HarperCollins), 2017, 179.

127 Lewis, *Surprised by Joy,* 179.

128 "Prayer to receive Jesus Christ as Savior", available on the website of wildatheart.org.

129 Lewis, *Mere Christianity,* 208–209.

130 Brook Ligertwood, "A Thousand Halleluiahs," retrieved from Apple.com. Released 2022

131 Lewis, *Surprised by Joy,* 179.

A free ebook edition is available with the purchase of this book.

To claim your free ebook edition:

1. Visit MorganJamesBOGO.com
2. Sign your name CLEARLY in the space
3. Complete the form and submit a photo of the entire copyright page
4. You or your friend can download the ebook to your preferred device

Print & Digital Together Forever.

Snap a photo

Free ebook

Read anywhere

CPSIA information can be obtained
at www.ICGtesting.com
Printed in the USA
JSHW032129100323
38793JS00001B/1

9 781631 959905